Rice & Curry

Rice&Curry

SRI LANKAN HOME COOKING

S.H. Fernando Jr.

HIPPOCRENE BOOKS, INC.
NEW YORK

Color photography by Susan Now.

Book and cover design by Acme Klong Design.

For more information, address:
HIPPOCRENE BOOKS, INC.
171 Madison Avenue
New York, NY 10016
www.hippocrenebooks.com

Cataloging-in-Publication data is available from the Library of Congress.

ISBN 13: 978-0-7818-1452-2

Printed in the United States of America.

For Ammi

ACKNOWLEDGEMENTS

Thanks to everyone who aided and inspired me on this journey—especially my mother Chandra Fernando, who raised me single-handedly with lots of love, patience, and all this incredible food! Thanks also to Uncle Cyril, Sid & Cynth, Siromi, and the rest of my family for their support. Special thanks to all my extended family in Sri Lanka, especially my aunts—Dora (RIP), Padma (RIP), Sita, Nalini (RIP), and Lalitha. Thanks also to Leela (RIP), Iraesha, Mihiri, Aunty Manel, and Aunty Reneira. Thanks to Sudath & Rushmi Perera, Dilukshi Nanayakkara, Aunty Stella, Mohara Dole. Thanks to Susan Now for the photos. Thanks to Priti Gress and the entire staff at Hippocrene Books for making this possible.

CONTENTS

Food has always intrigued and delighted me. One of my most vivid memories as a child, in fact, is climbing up on the kitchen counters to scour the cupboards for cookies or other goodies and stumbling upon an endless assortment of jars containing my mother's spices. This was my first introduction to cinnamon, coriander, cumin, nutmeg, cardamom, cloves, paprika, cayenne pepper, saffron, and much more. These spices seemed almost magical to me because I knew they were the secret ingredients my mother used to make our food taste so good. I remember curiously sniffing at the contents; poking a stubby finger in; dabbing a little on my tongue; and reveling in the different colors, flavors, smells, and textures. The moment of awakening for my taste buds had arrived.

Like any child my undeveloped palate veered towards Chef-Boyardee, Swanson, or McDonald's, but not because I didn't like my mother's cooking. A native of Sri Lanka, she prepared a pot of fluffy basmati rice and various meat and vegetable curries a couple of times a week. This is the food that stands out most in my mind. Sometimes I would watch her in the kitchen as she used a medieval-looking grater to scrape the succulent white "meat" out of a freshly split coconut, or ground spices together with a traditional stone mortar and pestle. Never measuring ingredients, she would simply add a pinch of this or a sprinkle of that to some chicken, fish, or vegetables to create a delectable dish whose enticing aroma wafted through our entire apartment. I always remember she was careful to close our bedroom doors, so the curry smell didn't permeate the bed sheets or the clothes that hung in our closets.

To the tongue, the flavors were always pungent and distinct—incomparable to any pot roast or meat loaf I ate at friends' houses. Growing up on this deliciously differ-

MAKING SAMBOL WITH
A GRINDING STONE

ent fare, it is hardly surprising that my tastes expanded to encompass other exotic flavors. Today my favorites include Vietnamese, Mexican, Malaysian, Indian, Middle Eastern, and Ethiopian foods. But still, nothing I have ever eaten quite compares to my mother's rice and curry.

In college, I came to appreciate Sri Lankan food even more, having had to suffer under mediocre institutional cooking for four years. Luckily, I could sometimes escape to my older brother's place, where, by this time, he was beginning to master the art of Sri Lankan home cooking. As the torch is inevitably handed down, so, too, did I acquire these skills over time. I discovered that not only was it infinitely easier to prepare a curry than I had ever expected, but this food also provided me with a crucial link to my identity as a Sri Lankan-American.

In *Rice & Curry: Sri Lankan Home Cooking*, I explore a rich culture and cuisine very near and dear to my heart. While conducting preliminary research for the first edition in 2007, I noticed a dearth of Sri Lankan cookbooks on the market— understandable considering this tiny island nation of some 22 million inhabitants could fit comfortably within the borders of Maine. Sri Lankan cuisine has also long been in the shadow of Indian food. But times are steadily changing. There are more Sri Lankan cookbooks than ever before. A new breed of consumers fed on a steady diet of Food Network and Cooking Channel, social media and the Internet, are expanding their horizons when it comes to food, seeking out different cuisines and trying out new things in the kitchen. Authentic restaurants in ethnic enclaves like Staten Island, New York, that boasts one of the largest communities of Sri Lankans living in the U.S., are catering to more than simply those of us who grew up on this food. In addition, ingredients such as coconut milk, lemongrass, and curry leaves are more widely available at national outlets such as Whole Foods. With its ease of preparation, substantial dietary benefits (using Ayurvedic herbs and spices), and, above all, unique flavors, Sri Lankan food is no longer the obscure cuisine that nobody has tried. It has finally received the recognition it deserves.

ADAM'S PEAK AT DAWN

As part of my initiation into the art of Sri Lankan cooking, I spent a year there, learning from the ground up—to gain a better understanding of the numerous spices and techniques used. I cooked practically every day, testing out the dishes included in these pages on members of my large extended family in Sri Lanka. Aunts, uncles, cousins, and friends, in fact, provided crucial insights and feedback, if not many of the recipes themselves. Since then, I have had more than a decade to tweak and perfect these dishes, cooking at supper clubs, special events, classes, and, of course, home.

For, at its heart, rice and curry is folk cooking, prepared and eaten every day at home. The exotic ingredients and complexity of flavors masks the ease of preparation. While you may be intimidated at first by the novelty of it all, I guarantee that in no time, you, too, can master this cuisine. Easy, step-by-step instructions and my notes and personal tips break down the process. Tantalizing photos will let you know what to expect for your toils. By using the suggested menus at the end of the book to put together a typical Sri Lankan table, you are in for a real taste of paradise. The journey is the destination, so please enjoy every step of the way!

INTRODUCTION

It speaks to the creativity, resourcefulness, and imagination of a people that utilizing the natural bounty of flora and fauna around them, they could create a cuisine as pleasing to the palate as it is healthy for mind and body and satisfying to the soul. Such is the promise of 'rice & curry,' as the national dish of Sri Lanka is known. Though understated in its description, this term encompasses a variety of preparations—from pungent to pacifying—served together as a single meal to create a complex tapestry of sights, smells, flavors, and textures, typically enjoyed with the fingers. Spanning the entire spectrum of tastes—from sweet, sour, bitter, savory, and spicy—a rice and curry meal usually includes at least one protein (meat or seafood), several vegetables, a salad, chutney, pickle, and crispy *papadum*—all anchored by an ample serving of rice.

The appeal of such a meal lies in its infinite permutations and combinations and, of course, just the right proportions when it comes to spicing. For

NAMIRIS (SCOTCH BONNET PEPPERS)

curry itself is not a single spice but a very sophisticated blend of coriander, cumin, cinnamon, cardamom, clove, fenugreek, black pepper, mustard seeds, turmeric, and, of course, the indispensable curry leaf *(Murraya koenigii)*. Such natural products—whether derived from seed, herb, fruit, root, leaf, or bark—have applications in the ancient Ayurvedic system of holistic health and were probably used as much for their medicinal and preservative properties as for flavor-enhancement, especially in the days before refrigeration. Additionally, there are as many recipes for the basic curry powder blend as there are cooks making it. The stinging heat of chili, despite popular notions to the contrary, does not make the list of principal ingredients (except in Jaffna curry powder), though it is inevitably added in the cooking process.

Sri Lankans, in fact, tend to lace their curries with generous doses of chili powder, whose popular analog in the west would be cayenne pepper. In addition to being a tonic in the tropics, encouraging one to sweat, and therefore cool off, chilis are also known for a myriad of health benefits including promoting good circulation. Their fiery nature remains a hallmark of the cuisine and one that distinguishes it from much tamer Indian fare, to which it is often compared. Incidentally, another major difference in the cuisines of these two close neighbors lies in Indian food's reliance on dairy—mostly in the form of ghee (clarified butter) and yogurt—while Sri Lankans favor coconut oil and coconut milk. The use of a non-animal fat makes Sri Lankan food less heavy and more vegan-friendly.

Just as curry does not refer to a single spice, so, too, are there a variety of curries. Red curries, which derive their name from the copious amount of chilies used, comprise the hottest variety. On the other end of the spectrum, white curries, named after their main ingredient, coconut milk, constitute the mildest, and are usually yellow-tinged from the addition of turmeric. Black curries require the addition of roasted, shredded coconut that imparts a smoky flavor, while the default color of most curries is brown, from the toasted spices.

In preparing curries, a good curry powder blend accounts for only part of the equation. Developing flavor is often a three-step process that involves marinating (especially meat dishes), slow cooking, and finally "tempering," a technique essential to Sri Lankan cuisine. This last process involves frying onions, curry leaves, and sometimes mustard seeds or even curry powder in oil before adding to the completed dish. Tempering a curry is often used to impart added flavor prior to a dish being served.

To the uninitiated, the preparation of Sri Lankan food may seem complex and time-consuming, but it is actually quick and simple. Of course, in the traditional Sri Lankan kitchen, usually located at the back of a house and equipped with an open hearth, clay pots, and such utensils as a mortar and pestle and *miris gala* or grinding stone to grind spices, it probably did take some time and effort to prepare a good meal. But the purpose of this book, in addition to demystifying the cuisine, is to prove that delicious dishes are well within everyone's reach. Our modern era of food processors, coffee grinders, and readily available ingredients like canned coconut milk, has allowed for a much greater ease of preparation.

Once you have made a batch of curry powder, roasting and grinding all the spices, for example, this mixture will last for several months in a sealed glass jar in the fridge. Other ingredients such as curry leaves or lemongrass are best used fresh and not in

GALLE FISH MARKET

STUPA

their dried or powdered form. In the name of authenticity, unrefined organic coconut oil is the oil of choice for most of these recipes, but any neutral vegetable oil offers a perfectly acceptable alternative. Sri Lankans also tend to use small red Bombay onions, which have an intense flavor, but yellow onions will suffice. When it comes to special ingredients like pandan leaf *(rampe)*, goraka *(Garcinia gamboge)*, and Maldive fish, you may not be able to find them at your local supermarket, but it is well worth the time to seek them out. To that end, I offer some online resources at the back of the book.

All the recipes in this book come from regular folks—usually family members and friends—and have been tested and perfected by yours truly. After all, Sri Lankan food represents folk cooking at its best. While I have enjoyed plenty of delicious meals at fancy restaurants as well as the little roadside "hotels" popular for Sri Lankan fast food, the best rice and curry I have eaten was at peoples' homes. Sri Lankan home cooks are known for not measuring ingredients, but rather adding a dash of this or a handful of that. So my challenge was to take their approximations and experiment until I was able to sufficiently reproduce what can only be described as authentic taste. Along the way, I tried to streamline the recipes and make them even healthier. I basically did all the hard work, so you don't have to. So please feel free to dive right in, and don't be intimidated by what you might consider exotic as you will soon be an expert. A new galaxy of flavors and techniques is yours to discover in this newly expanded and improved edition of *Rice & Curry: Sri Lankan Home Cooking*. Happy cooking and good eating!

ROADSIDE KADE (STORE)

A BRIEF HISTORY OF THE RESPLENDENT ISLE

SIGIRIYA (LION'S ROCK)

Situated in the Indian Ocean, this teardrop-shaped island just off the southernmost tip of India has been known since antiquity by such names as *Serendib*, The Resplendent Isle, Isle of Delight, Isle of Gems, the "pearl of the Indian Ocean," or simply *Taprobane* (meaning "paradise" in ancient Greek). While evidence of primitive human life there can be traced back some 1,750,000 years to ancestors of the island's aboriginal people or *Veddahs*, the first major literary and historical reference to the island appears in the great Hindu epic, *The Ramayana* (circa. 500 BCE). This story tells of the god

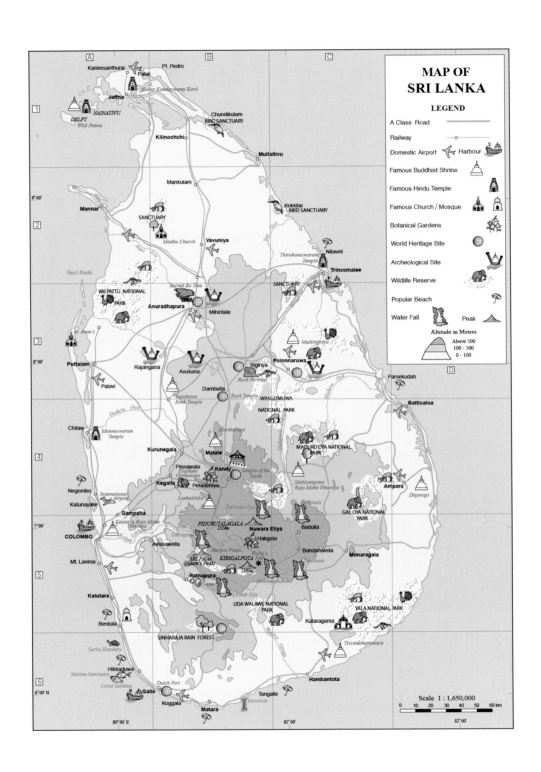

MAP OF
SRI LANKA
LEGEND

A Class Road
Railway
Domestic Airport   Harbour
Famous Buddhist Shrine
Famous Hindu Temple
Famous Church / Mosque
Botanical Gardens
World Heritage Site
Archeological Site
Wildlife Reserve
Popular Beach
Water Fall   Peak
Altitude in Metres
Above 500
100 - 500
0 - 100

A   B   C

Kankesanthurai   Pt. Pedro
Palali
Nallur Kandaswamy Kovil
Jaffna
NAINATIVU
DELFT   Chundikulam
Wild Ponies   BIRD SANCTUARY

Kilinochchi

Mankulam
Mannar   Kokkilai
SANCTUARY   BIRD SANCTUARY
Madhu Church   Vavuniya
Pearl Banks   Thirukoneswaram   Nilaveli
                              Temple   Trincomalee
WILPATTU NATIONAL   SANCTUARY
PARK   Sacred Bo Tree
St. Anne's   Anuradhapura   Medirigiriya
               Mihintale
Puttalam   Polonnaruwa
               Rajangana   Avukana   Sigiriya
Palavi   Dambulla   Rock Fortress
               Suparhawa   Rock Temple   Parsekudah
Chilaw   Rock Temple   WASGOMUWA
Munneswaram   NATIONAL PARK   Batticaloa
Temple   Atavihariya
Kurunegala   Matale
               Pinnawala   MADURU OYA NATIONAL
               Elephant   PARK
Negombo   Orphanage   Kandy   Temple of the
International   Tooth
Airport   Kegalla   Peradeniya   Ampara
Katunayake   Lankatilaka   Mahiyangana   Digavapi
Gampaha   Kurundu Oya   Raja Maha Viharaya
Kelaniya Raja Maha   GAL OYA NATIONAL
Viharaya   PARK
COLOMBO   PIDURUTALAGALA
               2524m   Nuwara Eliya
Avissawella   Hakgala   Badulla
Mt. Lavinia   Horton Plains   Bandarawela
          SRI PADA   KIRIGALPOTA   Monaragala
          (Adam's Peak)   2395m
Kalutara   Ratnapura   Gems
          Kirindi Ela
Bentota   UDA WALAWE NATIONAL
          PARK   YALA NATIONAL PARK
Turtle Hatchery   SINHARAJA RAIN FOREST   Kataragama
Marina Sanctuary   Hikkaduwa   Tissamaharamaya
Coral Gardens   Dutch Fort
          Galle   Hambantota
Koggala   Tangalle   Blowhole
          Matara

Scale 1 : 1,650,000
0   10   20   30   40   50   60 km

80° 00' E   81° 00'   82° 00'
9° 00'
8° 00'
7° 00'
6° 00' N

ANCIENT BUDDHA STATUE

Rama's conquest of Lanka, as it was then called, in 3000 BCE after Lanka's demon king, Ravana abducts Sita, his wife. Rama sends the monkey god Hanuman to rescue her, and while successful, he supposedly burns down the island in the process.

Myth and legend further meld with historical fact in *The Mahavamsa* ("Great Genealogy"), a Sri Lankan text compiled in the ancient Pali language in the sixth century BCE, in which King Vijaya, the grandson of a kidnapped Indian princess and an amorous lion becomes the first ruler of the Sinhalese people. From both accounts, we get an impression of a beautiful island rich in natural resources and already host to a flourishing civilization five hundred years before Christ. Buddhism found a foothold in Sri Lanka very early on, in 306 BCE, and it was here that the oral teachings of the Buddha, known as the *Tripitaka*, were first committed to writing, and soon adopted by royalty and the masses alike.

By virtue of its location on eastern trading routes, Sri Lanka has long been visited by Arab merchants, Malay seamen, and even Chinese emissaries. While most of the island's early history played out as a power struggle between Aryan kings (descended from northern India) and Dravidian invaders (from southern India), the character of Sri Lanka changed drastically with the arrival of the European colonial powers—beginning with the Portuguese in the 16th century (1505-1658), and continuing with the Dutch (1640-1796), and finally the British (1796-1948). Not coincidentally, western interest in the tiny island had a lot to do with the robust trade in

NINE ARCHES BRIDGE, ELLA

spices—especially cinnamon, which was a precious commodity traded with Egypt as far back as 1400 BCE. In addition to introducing Christianity into this predominantly Buddhist nation, the Europeans brought with them their own languages, customs, and cultural biases, which left an indelible impression on the local populace. They also left an infrastructure of roads and railways along with institutions, such as the parliamentary form of government, that have lasted into the present day.

Sri Lanka finally gained her independence from the British in 1948. Today, despite having one of the lowest per capita incomes, it boasts one of the highest standards of living in all of Southeast Asia, as well as a 90% literacy rate. It ranks third behind only India and China in the production of tea. Other exports include rubber as well as crops such as rice, coconuts, and, not surprisingly, spices (cinnamon, cardamom, cloves, nutmeg). Brilliant gemstones—blue sapphires, star sapphires, cats' eyes, and moonstones—comprise another one of Sri Lanka's natural treasures.

Of its 22 million inhabitants, Buddhist Sinhalese comprise a majority of 74%; the largely Hindu Tamils 13%; Muslims (descended from Arab merchants and Malay

RICE & CURRY

workers imported by the Dutch) 7%; and Christian Burghers (the mixed-race descendants of Europeans) round out this multi-ethnic, multi-religious society. This diverse populace has largely lived together in peace until simmering Tamil-Sinhala tensions sparked riots in 1983 that lead to conflict, unrest, and a 30-year struggle that was only resolved in May 2009 with the defeat of the terrorist group known as the Tamil Tigers. With the war now a page from the past, Sri Lanka may take its place, once again, as the resplendent isle—a place of dramatic sunsets and golden beaches, lush jungles and towering highlands, green paddy fields and tea plantations, a friendly and humble populace, and an amazing cuisine.

RICE & CURRY

Isle of Smiles

SRI LANKA:
A PRIMER

Though Sri Lanka has three official languages—Sinhalese, Tamil, and English—a visitor need not speak any one of them to get along just fine here. That's because locals are well-versed in the universal language of the smile. Whether in town or country, on the beach, or in the mountains, one will encounter an abundance of smiles, along with the good vibes that accompany them. After all, Sri Lanka prides itself as a welcoming destination where kindness and hospitality are the default settings of its people. A smile, therefore, means much more than a simple greeting. It's their way of saying, *"Thank you for taking the time and trouble to visit our beautiful island. Make yourself at home and enjoy the delights we have to offer."* And since smiles are infectious, you'll be beaming right back.

ESSENTIAL TRAVEL INFO

TIME ZONE: Sri Lanka is 5.5 hours ahead of Greenwich Mean Time (GMT + 5.5) and 11.5 hours ahead of Eastern Standard Time (EST) in the U.S. (EST + 11.5). They do not observe Daylight Savings Time.

VOLTAGE REQUIREMENTS:
230/240 volts AC; 50 Hz.
Both round and rectangular 2- or 3-pin plugs are the norm.

CURRENCY: Sri Lankan Rupee; Credit cards are accepted in urban areas; ATMs are readily available in urban areas.

INTERNET: High-speed Internet service is readily available in urban areas, but not as much in rural areas.

CELL PHONES: If you are visiting for an extended stay, think about getting a local SIM card (SL Telecom or Dialog), which is much cheaper than a roaming plan.

TIPPING: 10% service is added to hotel and restaurant bills, but anything additional is appreciated—especially for drivers/cabbies.

WHEN TO GO

Though the official tourist season runs from December to April, there is never a bad time to visit Sri Lanka, as it lies roughly 373 miles north of the Equator and enjoys average yearly temperatures between 82° to 86° F. There are two monsoon seasons affecting different parts of the island. The southwest monsoon season runs between May and July, while the shorter northeast monsoon season only runs from December to January. But thanks to climate change, even these predictable patterns have been interrupted.

GETTING THERE AND GETTING AROUND

Plenty of international carriers fly to Sri Lanka. Emirates, Qatar, and Kuwait Airlines all offer flights from the U.S. routed through the Middle East. Sri Lankan Airlines, Air India, Kingfisher, Lufthansa, KLM, and Swissair fly direct from major cities in Europe. Thai Airlines, Cathay Pacific, Malaysian, and Quantas are also options if you are flying from the opposite direction.

BUDDHA IN A LOCAL TEMPLE

RICE & CURRY

STORE AT NIGHT

WHERE TO STAY

Around the island, there is no shortage of hotels ranging from five star to budget. Air B&B also provides a good option. Visit the official site of Sri Lankan tourism, www.srilanka.travel, for more suggestions and information on holiday homes, guesthouses, boutique hotels, econo-lodges, and luxury apartments for rent.

Once on the island, there are a variety of ways to get around. Metered trishaws (or tuk-tuks) offer the best option for getting around town, though commuter buses are the cheapest. If you are planning a road trip, you can hire a car and driver for about US $25/day. Trains also provide the best option for intercity travel, offering 1st, 2nd, and 3rd class fares. Consult the Sri Lankan railways site (www.railway.gov.lk) for schedule and fare info.

CHANGING MONEY

Though a variety of Sri Lankan banks are available to change foreign currency into rupees at the official rates, you will get the best rates at so-called "black market" spots that locals prefer. Several of these are clustered together on the Galle Road in Wellewatta, including Prassana Money Exchange (57 Galle Rd), Royal Money Exchange (57 Galle Rd), and Swiss Money Exchange (87 Galle Rd). Another option is York St. in the vicinity of Pettah market which has a Swiss Money Exchange (51-B York St.), Royal Money Exchange (51-C York St.), and International Exchange (53-B York St.). You will get the best rates on $100 bills in pristine condition.

SAFETY AND HEALTH CONCERNS

Since the end of the long-standing conflict in May 2009, Sri Lanka had been relatively peaceful until the Easter bombings of 2019, carried out by Muslim extremists, who targeted several churches and tourist hotels. While street crime and violent crime are negligible, common sense suggests that you always keep your money in a secure place and don't carry more than you need. Other cardinal rules in the tropics include: Staying hydrated with plenty of bottled water, and never drinking tap water unless boiled; avoiding ice and juices in places with questionable hygiene; wearing sunscreen; using mosquito repellent to avoid being feasted upon. Those with sensitive stomachs, who are not accustomed to eating spicy food, might also want to bring antacid or anti-diarrheal medicine.

PEACOCK CROSSING

MEDICAL FACILITIES

If you do happen to fall sick in Sri Lanka, excellent and very affordable medical and dental care are readily available. Colombo has many private hospitals that offer a quality of care comparable to that in the west for a fraction of the cost. As you travel further from the capital, however, the same does not hold true.

POINTS OF INTEREST

For a tiny tropical island, Sri Lanka is brimming with enough attractions to satisfy anyone from the most ardent adventurer to the laziest beach bum. Whether it is sports, shopping, sightseeing, or just soaking up some rays, the following list provides a brief rundown of what's worth checking out on the island.

THE BEACHES Relaxing or rollicking in the sun, surf, and sand is probably the number one reason many tourists visit Sri Lanka each year. In fact, going "down south," is local parlance for a vacation at one of Sri Lanka's picturesque beaches. Only a couple hours south of Colombo, **Beruwala**, **Bentota**, and **Hikkaduwa**, have long been home to many fine resorts. Three hours south, past the southern city of Galle—known for its well-preserved 17th-century Dutch fort—you will find such beach towns as **Unawatuna**, **Ahangama**, and **Weligama**, which have become popular, tourist-friendly destinations in recent years offering many great hotels, restaurants, and activities. Further along you can go whale watching in **Mirissa**. Also think about heading to the pristine east coast, known for its white sand and blue waters. **Arugam Bay** offers an idyllic haven for surfers and snorkelers. Further up the east coast are the towns of **Batticaloa** and **Trincomalee**, whose natural harbor provides for a whole host of aquatic activities including dolphin watching. Don't skip the north either, where you can check out some of the amazing beaches and lagoons around **Jaffna**, and the northernmost town of **Point Pedro**.

BEACH AT AHANGAMA

DAMBULLA CAVES

HISTORICAL SITES Sri Lanka is home to eight UNESCO World Heritage sites, four of which happen to be in the north central part of the island in an area called the 'Cultural Triangle.' These include the sacred city of Anuradhapura, the ancient capital of Polonnaruwa, the caves of Dambulla, and the Sigiriya rock fortress. Located about 128 miles from Colombo, Anuradhapura was a major Buddhist center dating back to the 4th century BC. In addition to numerous Buddha statues, the site is famous for its ancient irrigation tanks as well as the Sri Maha Bodhi, which was grown from the original tree under which the Buddha attained enlightenment. Built in the 12th century AD, Polonnaruwa is known as one of Sri Lanka's ancient capitals, and the home to many pyramid-like dagobas or stupas that house Buddhist relics. Nearby stands the massive rock fortress of Sigiriya and the colorful painted caves of Dambulla. Typically, a five-day trip is sufficient to cover all these sites. Galle contains another UNESCO archaeological site in its 17th-century Dutch Fort, which has been recently restored to its former glory with the addition of several boutique hotels. The ancient hill city of Kandy stakes its claim as the seat of the last Sri Lankan kingdom as well as the location of the Dalada Maligawa (Temple of The Tooth), which supposedly houses Buddha's tooth relic.

GOLDEN TEMPLE DAMBULLA

WILD ELEPHANT

UPCOUNTRY TEA FIELDS

NATURE Sri Lanka's natural beauty and wildlife are unmatched. From national parks to botanical gardens, travel in any direction outside the bustling capital of Colombo and find yourself in a new world of wonder. From the 7,358-foot peak of *Sri Pada* (**Adam's Peak**), located in the central highlands, to the **Pinnawela Elephant Orphanage**, a short drive from Kandy, fully immerse yourself in the countryside to truly appreciate Sri Lanka's true untouched splendor. As far as national parks go, **Yala**, in the south, and **Kaudulla** in the northeast boast the greatest number of animal species including herds of elephant, sloth bears, and leopards. Or you could opt for a walk through the **Royal Botanical Gardens** of Peradeniya (outside Kandy). A visit to the numerous tea estates outside of Kandy and Nuwara Eliya, in the central highlands, also provides a delightful hill country excursion.

ECO-TOURISM Tourism to regions of ecological interest has grown exponentially in the last several years, and true nature lovers visiting Sri Lanka should be sure not to miss two sites in particular—the **Sinharaja Rainforest Reserve**, a UNESCO World Heritage site located in the southwest of the island, and **Knuckles Conservation Forest**, located near the central highlands. Consult the following two websites specifically geared to answer further questions on eco-tourism in Sri Lanka: The Sri Lanka Eco Tourism Foundation (www.ecotourismsrilanka.net) and Eco Team Sri Lanka (www.srilankaecotourism.com)

TOQUE MACAQUE MONKEY

PUBLIC HOLIDAYS AND FESTIVALS

POYA Each month's full moon day is commemorated by a Buddhist public holiday in Sri Lanka with banks and offices closed, and meat and alcohol unavailable for purchase (outside of hotels where most foreigners stay). The Vesak Poya in May is especially significant marking Lord Buddha's birth, enlightenment, and death, which is celebrated by a festival of lights when people make all manner of paper lanterns.

ALUTH AVURUDU The Sinhala and Tamil new year is generally celebrated in mid-April.

ESALA PERAHERA In August, a huge nighttime procession of elephants, dancers, drummers, fire-eaters, and acrobats marks this popular Kandy festival in which the sacred Buddha tooth relic is brought out of its home in the Dalada Maligawa Temple.

THAI PONGGAL A Tamil harvest festival that occurs in mid-January.

MAHA SIVARATHI (GREAT NIGHT OF SHIVA) A Tamil festival honoring Lord Shiva that occurs around February/March.

DEEPAVALI Also known as **Diwali** or the **Festival of Lights**, this is one of the bigger Hindu festivals. The date is dependent on the lunar/solar Hindu calendar, but usually occurs around October/November.

GALLE LITERARY FESTIVAL The island's premier literary event, featuring authors from home and abroad, occurs at the end of January.

HIKKADUWA BEACH FESTIVAL A more recent four-day beach festival featuring food, fun, and international deejays occurs at the end of July.

TEMPLE OF THE TOOTH, KANDY

GALLE FORT RAMPARTS

LION'S ROCK STAIRS

SHOPPING

Colombo is a shopper's delight for those in search of bargains and just the right souvenir of their trip. Whether it be precious gemstones, beautiful batiks and textiles, or some premium Ceylon tea, there is certainly something for everyone here. In addition to the broad range of cultural items found at government run establishments such as **Lak Sala** and **Lak Medura**, take a trip to Colombo's biggest department store, **Odells**, for just about anything else.

In addition to several major western-style malls or shopping centers, including Liberty Plaza and Crescat Mall, there are several independent stores that should not be missed. For textiles, housewares, and hand-loomed clothes, visit **Barefoot**, a well-known shop on the bustling Galle Road started by local designer Barbara Sansone. Housed in her renovated former home complete with a spacious backyard that has been converted into a café/restaurant, you can have a quiet drink or bite to eat while recovering from shopping. **Paradise Road** is another of Colombo's great finds for a truly unique gift or souvenir. From incense and candles to glasses and dishware, this store will also ship some of its heavier items directly to your home, so you won't have to lug it back. In a similar vein, the **Gallery Café**, located in the former home of renowned Sri Lankan architect Geoffrey Bawa has knick-knacks that you will not find anywhere else such as stationery made of Elephant dung.

A Cornucopia of Spices and Other Essential Ingredients

ASAFETIDA (PERUNKAYAM)

A member of the parsley family, asafetida features more prominently in South Indian and Tamil cuisine. The milky juice obtained from the root is dried to form a resinous brown mass that is more potent than the readily available powdered form. Due to its strong, sometimes offensive odor, reminiscent of fresh garlic, this is an ingredient to be used in moderation. In fact, just a pinch is sufficient. Asafetida is most often used in the preparation of dal (legumes) both as a flavoring and for its anti-flatulence properties.

BLACK MUSTARD SEEDS (ABBA)

About 1mm in diameter and actually dark brown in color, these tiny round seeds are derived from a plant that is a member of the cabbage family. While odorless, they reveal a pungent taste when chewed. Roasted, they take on a grayish hue, a pleasant nutty smell, and are far less pungent. Used in a variety of Sri Lankan dishes from pickles and chutneys to dal and mallun, the seeds are also supposed to be a good digestive. Black mustard seeds should not be confused with lighter-colored varieties, which are used to make the popular condiment mustard.

BLACK PEPPERCORNS (GAMMIRIS)

Peppercorns, the dried fruit (berries) of the pepper plant, are probably one of the most widely used spices in the world. They can be black, white, green, or red depending on the time of harvest and method of processing. Native to the Malabar Coast in southern India, pepper became one of the most important spices of antiquity, leading to the opening of trade routes between east and west. Today, pepper is produced throughout Southeast Asia. While adding a subtle boost to food, its flavor is not as pronounced as the kick from a chili. Peppercorns are best used freshly ground in a peppermill.

CARDAMOM *(ENASAL)*

The dried whole fruit of the cardamom plant, a member of the ginger family, is a distinctive spice in Sri Lankan cuisine. Native to southern India and Sri Lanka these elliptical green pods house black seeds. There is also a black variety that is used in Indian food. In the Middle East and parts of Africa, cardamom is most often used to flavor tea or coffee. After saffron and vanilla, it is considered the "third most expensive spice" in the world reflecting its wide popularity and usage. As the ground black seeds lose their flavor quickly, the cardamom pod is best used whole. The greener the pod, the more fragrant.

CAYENNE PEPPER POWDER/ CHILI POWDER (MIRIS KUDU)

Derived from grinding dried red chilies to a fine powder, chili powder is practically synonymous with the cayenne pepper powder used in the west. It should not, however, be confused with paprika, which shares its reddish hue but lacks any kick. Chili powder, which provides the heat in most Sri Lankan curries, should be regulated accordingly to suit everyone's palate. In moderate amounts, it promotes good circulation and digestion.

CINNAMON *(KURUNDU)*

As the cinnamon tree, a member of the laurel family, is native to Sri Lanka, it is only natural that this spice would find its way into a variety of dishes. Cinnamon is harvested by scraping the tree's inner bark to form quills that are typically used whole, but can be ground into powder as well. In the west, it is most often used in desserts. But in Sri Lanka it's sweet, warming flavor complements everything from fragrant biriyanis to fiery curries. It is also an ingredient in curry powder.

CLOVES (KARABUNATI)

Together with cardamom, dried cloves are a popular spice in Sri Lankan cuisine. Since these tiny flower buds pack a fragrant punch as well as a sharp, intense flavor, they should be used judiciously so as not to overpower other spices. Typically, one or two whole cloves are used during the making of a curry and removed afterwards. In Sri Lanka, toothpaste and mouthwash are made with clove oil for its powerful antiseptic properties.

CORIANDER SEEDS
(KOTTAMALLI)

Similar in appearance to its close cousin, parsley, the coriander plant can be used for its leaves, fruit (often called seeds), and roots, each of which possess a very distinct flavor. The dried, roasted fruit comprises one of the main ingredients of curry powder. The fresh leaves, often known as Chinese parsley or cilantro, are popular in Mexican, Thai, and Indian cooking, but rarely used in Sri Lanka. The taste of coriander seeds can be described as warm, nutty, and almost citrus-like. Sri Lankans make a tea from the powder that is used as a remedy for colds or fever.

CUMIN *(SUDURU)*

Cumin is a popular spice the world over except in the west, where it is often confused with caraway seeds, which it resembles. Another member of the parsley family, the strongly aromatic cumin fruits (called seeds) figure prominently in the multi-spice blend known as curry powder. They are usually toasted or fried in ghee or oil to enhance their sharp flavor and must be used judiciously so as not to override the other flavors of a curry. It is better to stock whole seeds to grind just before use to preserve its distinct aroma.

FENNEL SEEDS. *See* Sweet cumin

FENUGREEK (*ULUHAL*)

A spice from antiquity known for its medicinal properties (as a remedy for flatulence), fenugreek seeds are brownish yellow in color and characterized by their bitter flavor, so used sparingly. The plant's fresh green leaves, prepared like spinach, are eaten as well, sometimes utilized in dishes such as crab curry. Fenugreek is rich in phosphate, calcium, and iron, and is also said to be good for lowering cholesterol.

Ayurveda
THE SCIENCE OF LIFE

Ayurveda, a Sanskrit term referring to the holistic system of medicine that originated in India between 2500 and 1500 BCE, literally translates to "the science of life." In Hindu mythology the development of this form of traditional medicine can be attributed to Dhanvantari, physician of the Gods. Based on the five elements—earth, water, fire, air, and ether—that make up the universe (the macrocosm) and thus by association the human body (the microcosm), Ayurveda involves practical applications along with a strong metaphysical component as well. According to its basic philosophy, a healthy metabolic system with good digestion and proper excretion leads to vitality and longevity. To this end, the emphasis is on preventing disease, rejuvenating the body, and extending the life span.

Diet and nutrition obviously play a major role in maintaining good health, and in Ayurveda food is medicine. All food is characterized by six tastes—sweet, sour, salty, bitter, pungent, astringent—that should be present at every meal to maintain balance. People fall under three different elemental energies or *doshas—vata* (air), *pitta* (fire), *kapha* (earth)—and while everyone possesses a unique combination of these three, they usually favor one. Depending on your dominant dosha, different foods—including herbs and spices—will exert either beneficial, harmful, or neutral effects on you. Ayurveda, in fact, is behind the preparation of many traditional dishes in India and Sri Lanka.

As a discipline that encompasses mind, body, and spirit, Ayurveda also includes such components as yoga, meditation, and massage. In Sri Lanka today, Ayurvedic tourism has grown in popularity as visitors come to spend time in Ayurvedic spas or retreats. Among locals, Ayurvedic medicine is still as respected as western medicine, and many, including myself, continue to see traditional healers or *Wedemathaya*, who prescribe herbal remedies or certain foods in lieu of drugs.

MACE *(WASA-VASI)* / NUTMEG *(SADIKKA)*

Nutmeg is the seed of an apricot-like fruit that is native to the Banda Islands, part of the famed "Spice Islands" in Eastern Indonesia. Mace is the *arillus*, or thin leathery covering that partially shrouds the seed. While the pulp of this fruit is used to make a jam in Indonesia, the rest of the world knows nutmeg and mace mainly in their powdered form. Strongly aromatic, both spices are mostly used in desserts in the west, while Sri Lankans use them as a delicate flavoring in certain curries.

RED CHILI (DRIED)
(VELLICHEMIRIS)

Red chilies are the most popular variety of chili found in Sri Lanka. Sun dried before use, their reddish color deepens, also ensuring a longer shelf life. The main source of heat in Sri Lankan curries, this chili is either used whole, crushed into flakes, or powdered. If you have a low heat tolerance, paprika, which has all the color and none of the kick, would be an appropriate substitute.

SAFFRON

Saffron holds the honor of being the most expensive spice in the world. The thin red strands are the stigma (style) or female sex organs of the *Crocus sativa flower* (a member of the iris family). It takes approximately 150,000 such flowers to produce 1 kilo of dried saffron, which explains its expense. Saffron's intense and unique fragrance and taste can be overpowering, so a little goes a long way.

SALT *(DIYA LUNU)*

In addition to being essential for all metabolic functions, salt is an ingredient used since antiquity to flavor and sometimes preserve food. Used judiciously, it brings out other flavors. In Sri Lanka, home chefs often keep a bowl of brine (salt and water) by the stovetop for this purpose.

SWEET CUMIN *(MADURU)* / *FENNEL SEED*

Otherwise known as anise in the west, these 'seeds' are actually the dried fruits of a plant from the parsley family. While the leaves and stalks of this plant are eaten as a vegetable in Europe, only the dried, toasted fruit is used for curries in Sri Lanka. Toasting tends to change the flavor profile from sweet to spicier, which is probably why it is a main ingredient in curry powder.

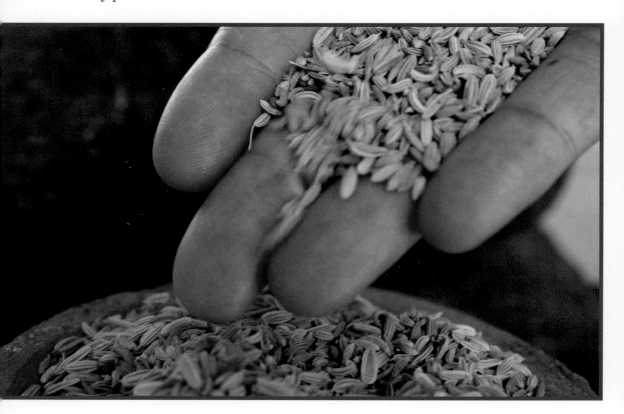

TURMERIC (KAHA)

A member of the ginger family, the turmeric rhizome resembles its cousin in its raw, root-like form. Fresh, it has a spicy, aromatic fragrance, but when dried, its odor becomes more medicinal. It is an ingredient used often, but sparingly, in Sri Lankan cooking. Along with its many culinary applications, it also has religious significance for Hindus, for whom its yellow hue represents the sun. Turmeric is also used as an antiseptic in Ayurvedic medicine.

Merits of the Coconut

In the trend-prone west, where consumption of coconut is relatively recent, and mostly limited to sweets, misconceptions abound about this delicious and very healthy fruit. For starters, the coconut has received a bad rap due to its high saturated fat content and the belief that it raises cholesterol levels. But, like avocado, it is not an animal fat, so those fats are beneficial. New studies are also showing some very promising results. While coconut oil, for example, does contain a high percentage of fat, approximately 50 percent of these fatty acids are in the form of lauric acid, a medium-chain fatty acid found in human breast milk. These fatty acids are not stored but sent directly to the liver and converted into energy, actually speeding up the body's metabolism and promoting weight loss. In addition, lauric acid, which is converted into monolaurin in the human body, is anti-viral, anti-bacterial, and anti-fungal, and scientists are finding it effective in treating HIV, herpes, and even common viruses like the flu. Studies have also shown that coconut oil reduces overall cholesterol levels if they are high and increases them if they are low. But don't take my word on it—do a little research for yourself. The information is out there. As Dr. Bruce Fife, author of *The Healing Miracles of Coconut Oil*, says, "Coconut oil is the healthiest oil on Earth." Since Sri Lankan cuisine is practically immersed in coconut milk and coconut oil, go ahead and indulge!

Other Essential Ingredients

COCONUT MILK / COCONUT OIL (POL KIRI/ POL THEL)

Since coconuts grow abundantly around the island, it makes sense that they are one of the essential elements of Sri Lankan cuisine. Shredding their white 'meat,' macerating it in water, and straining it yields coconut milk, an ingredient in most curries. Boiling down this milk yields coconut oil, which is the primary fat used for cooking (recommended for use in all recipes here). In addition, the sap from the coconut flowers is also used to make toddy and treacle, a sweet syrup, while the hard shells are used to make twine, utensils, and tools.

CURRY LEAVES (*KARAPINCHA*)

Not to be confused with the curry plant of southern European origin, the curry tree is indigenous to India. One of the essential flavors of Sri Lankan cuisine, curry leaves are an ingredient without equal (do not even consider substituting bay leaves). They are used both fresh and fried in practically every savory Sri Lankan dish, including rice. Buy the leaves fresh from any Indian store because the dried variety just does not compare. They may be stored in the fridge for a few days, but do not freeze well.

GARLIC (SUDULUNU)

A member of the onion family, garlic is another flavor enhancer popular worldwide. Its characteristic strong odor lessens significantly when cooked making it the perfect complement to ginger, pepper, chilies, and other spices used in Sri Lankan curries. In addition, garlic contains a whole host of health benefits from boosting the immune system to lowering cholesterol.

GINGER (INGURU)

Ginger ranks among the most important and popular spices in the world. A fleshy, white rhizome covered by a thick light-brown skin, the pungent odor and flavor of fresh ginger is unmistakable. In Sri Lanka, ginger is mostly used cooked, not raw, allowing the warming spicy flavor to give way to a mild, rich taste that blends perfectly with fried garlic and onion. Ginger is also beneficial for digestion and stomach ailments.

GREEN CHILI (AMU MIRIS)

The pre-ripened stage of the red chili, fresh green chilies provide an added kick to Sri Lankan curries. Though it is almost unthinkable to have any type of Asian food without heat, this plant, along with other New World crops like the tomato and potato, was introduced to Africa and Asia by the Portuguese. Before its arrival, people in this part of the world only had black pepper to add a kick to their food.

LIME (DEHI)

A lime is to Sri Lankan cooking as a lemon is to Mediterranean cuisine. Used as a souring agent in the preparation of some curries, lime is also squeezed on many dishes before serving to give them added zing.

GHEE

Ghee or clarified butter adds a very rich flavor to rice and curry and is suitable for cooking at higher temperatures. It can be made by simply melting butter and separating the clear residue from the solids. While more commonly used in Indian cooking, it is indispensable for a dish like biriyani.

GORAKA (GARCINIA GAMBOGE)

Goraka is a popular souring agent/acid in Sri Lankan cuisine. These kidney-shaped fruits, black when dried, are placed in warm water to soften up. They may be added whole to a curry and also ground into a paste. You should be able to source this ingredient online or at any Sri Lankan store. It also comes as a ready-made paste with salt and garlic included. As this fruit is native to Sri Lanka, if you can't find a source the best substitute for it would be tamarind.

LEMONGRASS (SERA)

While Thai food is most associated with lemongrass, Sri Lankans also use the sliced white stalks of this indigenous grass to flavor their curries—albeit in more subtle ways. Typically, only a small piece will be used so as not to overwhelm other ingredients. Fresh lemongrass used to be hard to find in the U.S., but today it is readily available at Whole Foods or any Asian market.

ONION (LUNU)

Classified as a vegetable of the genus *Allium*—along with garlic, scallions, leeks, and chives—the onion is probably the oldest and most widely used flavor enhancer, mentioned in the Old Testament as well as the clay tablets from Mesopotamia. A raw onion's pungent odor and taste mellows upon cooking—sometimes to the point of becoming sweet. Sri Lankans slow-cook them in practically every kind of curry, as well as adding them fried along with curry leaves at the end of a preparation in a unique process known as "tempering." Shallots are also used in Sri Lankan cooking for a finer, less pungent flavor.

MALDIVE FISH *(UMBALAKADA)*

Maldive fish refers to bonito tuna that has been boiled, dried in the sun until rock-hard, and shredded. As an ingredient specific to Sri Lankan cuisine, it is unlikely that you will find it outside of a store selling Sri Lankan products. It might be worth going out of your way to find it, however, as it adds great flavor and consistency to such dishes as *mallung* and coconut *sambol*. A suitable substitute would be the small, dried shrimp found in Asian grocery stores.

PANDAN LEAF *(RAMPE)*

Known as the "screw pine" or "umbrella tree" in English, pandan leaves are always used fresh or slightly withered (when their pleasant, nutty aroma is most evident). While some Asian cultures—including the Thais, Malaysians, and Indonesians—use the leaves primarily to flavor rice, Sri Lankans also use them in many curries. Because of the scarcity of fresh pandan leaf in the west and the subtle flavor it imparts, this ingredient is optional in most recipes here. It may be substituted by its essence, known as *Toey*, which might be sourced at a Thai store.

TAMARIND *(SIYAMBALA)*
Originally from East Africa, tamarind has become a fruit known all over the tropics for its intensely tart flavor. The pea-shaped pods may be eaten raw, but for cooking purposes only the pulp is used—usually soaked in water and strained of seeds and fiber. Utilized heavily in South Indian and Tamil cooking, alongside plenty of chilies, tamarind gives this food its characteristic hot and sour taste and dark color. In Sri Lanka, it is used as a souring agent in a wide variety of meat and fish curries. It can also be used as a substitute for goraka.

RECIPES

RICE & CURRY

SPICE BLENDS

Practically every country in Asia has their own version of the spice blend commonly known as curry powder. In Sri Lanka, where curries are commonplace, several commercial varieties exist, yet many home cooks prefer to whip up their own batch. Though the basic ingredients are the same, proportions and special additions can vary between households. One thing, however, is certain: The store-bought kind cannot compete with the flavor and aroma of homemade.

Making curry powder in Sri Lanka involves buying whole, raw spices in bulk. First, they must be washed and sun-dried in handwoven, palm frond baskets before being taken to a grinding mill to be roasted and ground. But, thankfully, one does not have to go to such great lengths to get a decent blend. You can purchase smaller packets of dry spices, pan-roast and grind them in a coffee grinder (dedicated for spices only), and store the blend in a glass jar in the refrigerator, where it will retain its essence for up to six months.

Curry

Today the term "curry" evokes a spice-laden dish with a rich sauce or gravy, but the etymology of the word has a mixed heritage. "Cury" comes from the Old English term for cooking, derived from the French *cuire*, meaning to cook, boil, or grill. It appears in the title of the first real English cookbook, "The Forme of Cury," commissioned by King Richard II in 1390—obviously long before British contact with Asia. Modern usage of the term "curry" can more likely be traced to the south Indian languages of Kannadan and Malayalam, in which the word *karil* is used to alternatively describe a mixture of spices as well as dishes of sautéed meat and vegetables. Similarly, in the Tamil language, *kari* means sauce. Under the Portuguese, who were the first European traders in South Asia, these terms morphed into "caril" and "carree," which eventually became "curry" in the British parlance. It should also be noted that the wok-shaped pan in which meals are prepared in India is called a karahi.

Despite great regional variations in Indian cooking styles, the British simply adopted "curry" as a generic term for any spicy dish with a thick sauce or gravy. They also invented curry powder as a means for exporting the dishes they fell in love with in India back to the homeland. While Indians are very familiar with masalas, or premixed spice mixtures, usually added at the end of the cooking process, the concept of curry powder was foreign to them. In the typical Indian kitchen, equipped with a grindstone, spices were usually ground and mixed to order, according to whatever dish was being prepared. But as the British came to think of all curries as variations on the same theme, they devised the concept of curry powder, which made it easier for cooks back in England to re-create those beloved Indian dishes.

Raw Curry Powder

This basic, unroasted spice mixture has a lighter color, milder flavor, and is generally used for vegetable curries. You may scale up from these amounts to make as much as you need.

3 tablespoons coriander seeds   1½ tablespoons fennel seeds
3 tablespoons cumin seeds   1 teaspoon turmeric powder

Grind ingredients together in coffee grinder and store in a glass jar in the fridge.

Jaffna Curry Powder

This version of curry powder comes from the northern, predominantly Tamil, part of the country. Since Tamil food is known for its heat, chilies are added directly to the mix.

4 ounces dry red chilies   2 sprigs curry leaves
8 tablespoons coriander seeds   2 tablespoons fennel seeds
2 tablespoons black peppercorns   1 tablespoon white cumin seeds
1 teaspoon turmeric powder   1 tablespoon fenugreek seeds

Place chilies, coriander seeds, peppercorns, turmeric, and curry leaves in a pan and dry roast until curry leaves are crisp. Remove from heat. Roast fennel seeds, white cumin seeds, and fenugreek seeds until golden brown. Mix all ingredients together and grind in a coffee grinder. Store in a glass jar in the fridge.

Roasted Curry Powder

This spice mixture, used for meat and fish curries, has a very complex, multidimensional flavor thanks to all the spices used and the fact that each is toasted, releasing their essential oils. The heat from a curry comes from chili powder (cayenne pepper powder) which is added separately to reach the desired heat.

1 tablespoon uncooked rice
4 tablespoons coriander seeds
2 tablespoons cumin seeds
2 tablespoons fennel seeds
2-inch (5-cm) cinnamon stick
½ teaspoon fenugreek seeds
1 teaspoon black peppercorns

1 teaspoon black mustard seeds
1 teaspoon turmeric powder
5 cardamom pods, shelled
5 cloves
2-inch (5-cm) piece pandan leaf (optional)
2 sprigs curry leaves

Toast each ingredient separately in a pan over medium heat, stirring often, until fragrant and browned (be careful not to burn). Remove from heat, cool, and grind together in a dedicated coffee grinder. Store in a glass jar in the fridge.

NOTE: If you are feeling lazy, no worries. I've done the work for you. You may purchase Skiz's Original Roasted or Raw Curry Powder at www.skizsoriginal.com.

SPICE BLENDS   53

SHORT EATS,
SNACKS &
STREET FOOD

As notorious snackers, Sri Lankans enjoy savory "short eats" any time of the day. These deep-fried treats, conveniently sold at bakeries or ubiquitous roadside stalls or *kades*, comprise a popular street food. More substantial snacks include deviled meats or seafood, which provide the perfect accompaniment to a cold beer. And after a night of drinking, *kotthu* roti, a combination of meat, veggies, eggs, and thin flatbread chopped up on a hot griddle and splashed with a curry gravy, usually hits the spot.

Beef, Mutton, Fish or Veggie Cutlets

These breaded, deep-fried cutlets, filled with your choice of meat, fish, or veggies, make the perfect finger food—suitable for a cocktail party or a savory bite with afternoon tea. This filling can also be used to make Beef, Fish, or Veggie Patties (page 59) and Mihiri's Chinese Rolls (page 60).

BEEF, MUTTON, FISH OR VEGGIE FILLING:

1 large potato
2 tablespoons oil
1 medium onion, finely diced
2 cloves garlic, minced
2-inch (5 cm) piece ginger, minced
2 to 3 green chilies, finely chopped
1 sprig curry leaves, chopped
½ pound (226 g) ground beef; or ½ pound (226 g) ground mutton; or 1 (15 oz./425 g) can of fish (tuna, salmon, or mackerel); or ½ head of cabbage, shredded and 2 medium carrots, shredded
1 teaspoon cayenne pepper powder
1 teaspoon raw curry powder
salt to taste
½ teaspoon ground black pepper
juice of lime (if making fish or veggie filling)

COATING:

1 cup all-purpose flour
1 beaten egg (with a little water added to thin it out)
2 cups (500 ml) panko breadcrumbs
oil for frying

PREPARE FILLING:

1. Wash, peel, and dice potato. Boil in salted water until soft (about 5 to 7 minutes). Drain and set aside.

2. Heat oil in pan. Fry onions, garlic, ginger, green chilies, and curry leaves until onions are translucent.

3. Add cooked potatoes, protein or shredded vegetables, and cayenne pepper powder, curry powder, salt and pepper. Toss well and sauté for 3 to 5 minutes, roughly mashing potato with spatula. Squeeze in lime juice if using, then set aside to cool.

CONTINUED

PREPARE CUTLETS:

4. When filling is cool, form into golf-ball-size balls. Roll in flour to coat; then egg mixture; and finally in the breadcrumbs.

5. Heat oil in a deep pan to 350 degrees F (175 degrees C) (oil should be deep enough to cover the cutlets).

6. Deep fry cutlets until golden brown. Remove to a sheet pan lined with paper towels and a wire rack to drain excess oil. Best served hot.

MAKES 15 TO 20 CUTLETS

Beef, Mutton, Fish or Veggie Patties

These cute little savory pastries are the mini-me of Jamaican patties and constitute a more flavorful (and spicier) version of the Spanish empanada or English Cornish Pasty. Though they are typically deep-fried, I like to bake mine in the oven for a healthier version.

FILLING

Beef, Mutton, Fish, or Veggie filling of choice (see page 57)

PASTRY DOUGH:

1 pound (454 g) all-purpose flour
1 teaspoon salt
3 egg yolks
4 tablespoons unsalted butter (cold), coconut oil, or shortening
dash of lemon juice
1 beaten egg (with a little water added)

1. Make filling of choice and let cool.

2. **PREPARE PASTRY DOUGH:** Put flour and salt in a bowl. Make a well in the center, add egg yolks, and mix well. Add butter or oil and lemon juice and knead with hands until dough comes together. Form into a ball, wrap in plastic, and set aside in fridge for about 30 minutes.

3. Roll pastry dough thin (about ⅛-inch to ¼-inch thick) on a floured surface. Use the mouth of a glass or small bowl to stamp out rounds about 4 to 5 inches in diameter.

4. Place 1 tablespoon of filling in center of round and slightly flatten. Wet one semicircle edge with water, and fold pastry over. Use teeth of fork to fuse the two edges together. Repeat with remaining filling and dough.

5. After all patties are made, preheat oven to 350 degrees F (160 degrees C). Place patties on ungreased baking sheet and brush exterior with egg wash. Bake for 15 to 20 minutes. Patties may also be deep-fried.

6. Cool on wire rack before serving.

MAKES 15 TO 20 PATTIES

Mihiri's Chinese Rolls

These tasty snacks got their name since they closely resemble the traditional egg roll. My aunt's neighbor Mihiri is like a one-woman factory when it comes to making them, dipping them in the batter with one hand and frying them with the other. Despite being somewhat labor-intensive, these crunchy breaded rolls surrounding a moist tasty filling are well worth your efforts.

FILLING:
Beef, Mutton, Fish, or Veggie filling of choice (see page 57)

BATTER:
2 cups (500 ml) all-purpose flour
2 eggs
1 cup (250 ml) water
½ teaspoon baking powder
salt to taste

OUTER COATING:
2 cups (500 ml) panko breadcrumbs
oil for frying

1. Make filling of choice and set aside to cool.

2. Combine all batter ingredients in a bowl and mix. It should have the consistency of pancake batter.

3. Heat pan and brush with oil. Once smoking, ladle one spoonful of batter onto pan and swirl around. Pancake should be about ⅛ inch (3 mm) to ¼ inch (6 mm) thick and 4 to 5 inches (11 to 13 cm) in diameter. Once bubbles form on surface, flip over and cook an additional 1 to 2 minutes. Set aside on a plate. Repeat process until you have 10 to 15 pancakes (you should have some batter left over to use in Step 5). **NOTE:** Brush pan with oil before making each pancake.

4. To assemble rolls, place 1 to 2 tablespoons of filling on the side of the pancake closest to you and spread into a line. Fold in the sides toward the center first, and starting with the edge closest to you, roll into a cigar shape. The moisture should create a natural seal.

5. When all the rolls are made, dip each roll in the batter again and coat with breadcrumbs.

6. Heat oil to 350 degrees F (177 degrees C) in a deep pan or wok. Working in batches, carefully immerse each roll and fry until golden brown. Remove to a wire rack on a sheetpan lined with paper towels to drain excess oil. Serve hot.

NOTE: These Chinese rolls may be assembled and stored (frozen) after the batter and breading stage. Then fry when ready to serve.

MAKES 10 TO 15 ROLLS

Spicy Lentil Fritters
Masala Vadai

A spicy Sri Lankan version of falafel, made with yellow split peas instead of chickpeas, this flavorful snack boasts a crisp exterior and moist middle, providing the perfect cure for the munchies.

2 cups (500 ml) yellow split peas
1 medium onion, chopped
2 to 3 green chilies, finely chopped
1 teaspoon fennel seeds

1 sprig curry leaves, chopped
salt to taste
oil for frying

1. Soak split peas in water for at least 8 hours, changing the water once. Rinse and drain. Reserve ¼ cup split peas and grind the rest to a smooth, thick paste in a blender or food processor (adding a little water as necessary). Add the reserved split peas back to this mixture.

2. Mix all other ingredients except the oil with the ground split peas.

3. Form mixture into golf-ball-size rounds. Slightly flatten each round using both cupped palms of your hands so the middle is thicker than the edges.
(**NOTE:** Wetting your hands ensures that the mixture does not stick to them.)

4. Deep fry in oil heated to 350 degrees F (177 degrees C) until golden brown.

5. Remove to wire rack lined with paper towels to drain excess oil. Serve immediately.

MAKES 15 TO 20 VADAI

Savory Donuts
Ulundu Vadai

Black gram *(Vigna mungo)* or *urad dal*, a member of the mung bean family, is a type of lentil grown in South Asia that packs a protein-filled punch. Deep frying makes them crispy on the outside, while light and airy on the inside. They taste great alone, but also pair well with yogurt or a side of coconut chutney.

1 cup (240 ml) split black gram or
  urad dal
1 medium onion, finely chopped
2 to 3 green chilies, finely chopped
1 sprig curry leaves, finely chopped

1 teaspoon black mustard seeds
¼ teaspoon baking powder
salt to taste
oil for frying

1. Cover and soak dal in water for at least 8 hours, changing the water at least once. Rinse and drain. Grind to a smooth, thick paste in food processor or blender (adding a little water as necessary).

2. Heat 2 tablespoons oil in a pan. Add onions, green chilies, and curry leaves, and fry until onions are translucent. Add mustard seeds and fry until they start to pop (about a minute).

3. Fold tempered ingredients into lentil mixture and add baking powder and salt to taste. Mix well.

4. Heat oil to 350 degrees F (177 degrees C) in a deep pan or wok. Using about 2 tablespoons of lentil mixture, form into a disk in the palms of your hands. Make a hole in the middle using a finger and carefully slide into the hot oil. (**NOTE:** Wetting the hands will prevent the mixture from sticking to them.)

5. Deep fry until golden brown, flipping once. Remove to a wire rack lined with paper towels to drain and cool slightly.

6. Serve immediately with yogurt or Coconut Chutney (page 192).

MAKES 10 TO 15 VADAI

Spicy Chickpeas
Kadala Thel Dala

A popular street food, these spicy treats typically come served in a cone made of newspaper. Easy to prepare as well as healthy and delicious, why not enjoy them at home instead of going for that bag of potato chips?

2 tablespoons coconut oil
1 small red onion, sliced
1 sprig curry leaves
1 teaspoon cumin seeds
1 teaspoon black mustard seeds
2 (14-ounce) cans chickpeas, rinsed
  and drained

¼ teaspoon turmeric powder
2 teaspoons chili flakes
salt to taste

1. Heat oil in pan. Add onion slices and curry leaves, and fry until onions are translucent. Add cumin seeds and mustard seeds and continue frying until mustard seeds start to pop (about a minute).

2. Add chickpeas, turmeric, chili flakes, and salt and toss to coat, sautéing for 2 to 3 minutes. Serve immediately.

MAKES 4 SERVINGS AS AN APPETIZER

Nimal's Deviled Beef/ Chicken/Pork

Deviled or "spiced" meats offer the perfect accompaniment to a cold beer. Similar in preparation to a Chinese stir-fry, this dish is a stand-alone finger food that has truly emerged as an island favorite. My late friend Nimal, a former cook turned tri-shaw driver, originally gave me this recipe.

1 pound (500 g) beef, chicken, or pork, cut into 1-inch cubes
½ teaspoon salt
½ teaspoon black pepper
1 to 2 teaspoons cayenne pepper powder
2 tablespoons soy sauce
1 teaspoon sugar
2 tablespoons oil
1 onion, sliced
3 cloves garlic, sliced

2-inch (5 cm) piece ginger, peeled and sliced into matchsticks
2 green chilies, sliced thin on the bias
2 Anaheim (capsicum) chilies, sliced thin on the bias
1 tomato, diced
2 tablespoons ketchup
1 teaspoon apple cider vinegar
½ inch (1.25 cm) cinnamon stick

1. Season meat with salt, pepper, cayenne pepper powder, 1 tablespoon soy sauce, and sugar and marinate for at least 1 hour.

2. Heat 1 tablespoon oil in frying pan and stir-fry meat 3 to 4 minutes until browned. Remove to a plate.

3. Heat remaining 1 tablespoon oil and fry onion slices, garlic, ginger, both chilies, and tomatoes until onions are translucent.

4. Add meat back into pan along with ketchup, remaining 1 tablespoon soy sauce, vinegar, and cinnamon stick.

5. Mix well and stir-fry for an additional 5 minutes to blend flavors. Serve immediately.

MAKES 4 SERVINGS AS AN APPETIZER

Deviled Shrimp or Squid

Seafood gets the 'deviled' treatment with this fiery snack. It is akin to a Chinese stir-fry but eaten without rice. Pairs perfectly with a cold beer.

1 pound (500 g) shrimp or squid
Salt to taste
½ teaspoon turmeric
2 tablespoons oil
1 medium onion, sliced
4 cloves garlic, sliced
1 teaspoon crushed fresh ginger
1 sprig curry leaves
1 tomato, diced

2 green chilies, sliced thin
  on the bias
2 Anaheim (Capsicum) chilies,
  sliced thinly on the bias
1 teaspoon cayenne pepper powder
1 to 2 teaspoon chili flakes
2 tablespoons ketchup
2 tablespoons soy sauce
juice of lime

1. Wash, shell and devein shrimp; or cut squid into 1-inch (2.5 cm) strips. Season with salt and turmeric and set aside.

2. Heat oil in frying pan. Sauté onions, garlic, ginger, and curry leaves for 2 to 3 minutes. Add tomatoes and both chilies and sauté 2 minutes more.

3. Add shrimp or squid, cayenne pepper powder, chili flakes, ketchup, and soy sauce, and stir-fry for 2 to 3 minutes until shrimp turns pink or squid becomes opaque. Be careful not to overcook. Add salt to taste.

4. Remove from heat, plate, and squeeze with lime before serving.

MAKES 4 SERVINGS AS AN APPETIZER

Fried Anchovies or Sardines
Hal Masso

In Sri Lanka, tiny fish known as sprats are lightly dusted with cornstarch and fried in hot oil for a quick snack. A sprinkle of salt and a squeeze of lime serves as a simple dressing. When I make this dish, I like to use a larger silver fish called *Salya*, about 4 inches long, that resemble small sardines. You must scale and degut them, but leave the heads and tails on, which get crunchy when fried. I also spike my cornstarch with salt, pepper, and a little cayenne pepper powder—or better yet Old Bay—to make them really pop. A plate of these washed down with some cold beers is the only ticket you need to transport you to a tropical beach somewhere.

1 pound small fresh fish, like
  anchovies or sardines
½ cup cornstarch
½ teaspoon salt
½ teaspoon pepper

1 tablespoon Old Bay seasoning
Oil for frying
Squeeze of lime juice
Salt to taste

1. Wash and clean fish. If using a bigger fish than anchovies, as I do, you'll have to scale them with a serrated paring knife and remove the guts.

2. In a shallow bowl, make a simple coating with the cornstarch, salt, pepper, and Old Bay (if using). Dredge all the fish, dusting off excess coating, and keep ready on a plate.

3. Heat oil to 350 degrees F (177 degrees C) in a small pot. Fry the fish in small batches until golden brown.

4. Remove to a wire-rack lined with paper-towels and set into a sheet pan. Sprinkle with salt to taste and squeeze on some lime juice. Serve immediately.

MAKES 4 SERVINGS AS AN APPETIZER

Kottu Roti

Arguably the most popular and iconic street food in Sri Lanka, this humble dish began as a way to repurpose leftovers. It's a mixture of chopped up meat, vegetables, curry, eggs, gravy, and flatbread—thus the name, 'kottu,' which means 'chop' in Tamil. Kottu comes together on a searing hot griddle, where everything is quickly tossed together with a pair of metal bench scrapers. The resulting clang creates a familiar sound across the island where the dish is enjoyed as a quick and cheap evening meal—even more appealing after a night of drinking. Personally, I'm not a big fan of the dish, and the late Anthony Bourdain echoed my sentiments when he likened it to "curried turkey stuffing," but that doesn't mean diddly to its legion of devotees. So, decide for yourself, and feel free to improvise and get creative at home. Of course, you'll need to make a portion of gothamba roti or simply use store bought flour tortillas as an acceptable substitute.

2 tablespoons oil
1 small onion, thinly sliced
1 carrot, peeled and grated
1 leek, cleaned, halved lengthwise, and sliced
2 scallions, sliced on the bias
2 green chilies, sliced on the bias

2 eggs, beaten (with salt and pepper)
1 portion curry (6- to 8-ounces), any variety (meat or veg), gravy reserved
2 gothamba rotis (page 102) or flour tortillas, cut into thin strips
Salt and pepper to taste

1. Heat 1 tablespoon oil in pan. When hot add onion, carrot, leek, scallions, and green chilies and stir-fry for 2 to 3 minutes until tender. Move to the side of pan.

2. Add the rest of the oil and allow to heat up for 30 seconds before pouring in the beaten eggs. Scramble eggs separately before incorporating with vegetables, stir-frying for another 30 seconds.

3. Add curry and use spatula to break it up and mix with vegetables. Stir-fry for a minute and add roti or tortilla strips and the reserved gravy. Mix everything well for another 2 minutes until it all comes together, seasoning with salt and pepper. Serve immediately.

MAKES 2 SERVINGS

ODIYAL KOOL

SOUPS & GRAVIES

Eating soup may seem counterintuitive in a sweltering tropical clime, but Sri Lankans often enjoy it as a light evening meal or to cool off since sweating turns the slightest breeze into instant air-conditioning.

Jaffna Seafood Soup
Odiyal Kool

This very substantial and spicy soup utilizes much of the bountiful seafood of coastal Jaffna, where it originated. Think gumbo thickened with Palmyra root flour, otherwise known as *odiyal*. Though difficult to source outside of Sri Lanka, it gives the soup its distinctive flavor, but an acceptable substitute would be half the amount of potato starch. You could even opt for a traditional roux from equal parts flour and butter. Jackfruit seeds are typically added to the mix, but they may be hard to source as well.

¼ pound (113 g) fish
¼ pound (113 g) squid
½ pound (226 g) shrimp
½ pound (226 g) crabs
½ cup green beans
4 ounces (125 g) manioc (yucca) or potato, peeled and boiled
¼ pound (113 g) spinach
½ cup (185 g) Palmyra root flour (*odiyal*) or ¼ cup potato flour/starch

3 tablespoons tamarind pods*
¼ pound (113 g) jackfruit seeds, chopped (optional)
1 teaspoon coarse sea salt
3 tablespoons raw rice
2 tablespoons cayenne pepper powder
4 dried red chilies
½ teaspoon turmeric powder
Salt to taste
Shredded coconut

1. **WASH AND CLEAN SEAFOOD:** Cut fish into bite-sized chunks, slice squid, shell shrimp, and quarter crabs.

2. **PREPARE VEGETABLES:** Cut green beans into 1-inch pieces; dice boiled manioc or potato; wash and chop spinach.

3. Soak Palmyra root flour in a cup of water for 10 minutes and strain. Repeat this three times to reduce bitterness.

4. Soak tamarind pods in a ½ cup of water, remove seeds and fiber, and strain.

5. Fill half a large pot with about 4 cups water, 1 teaspoon coarse sea salt, and rice and bring to a boil.

6. Add fish, squid, shrimp, crabs, and beans and cook for 15 to 20 minutes. Add manioc and jackfruit seeds (if using) and cook for an additional 5 minutes.

7. In a separate bowl mix Palmyra root flour or potato starch, tamarind water, cayenne pepper powder, dried red chilies, and turmeric into a thick paste. Add paste to seafood broth, mix well and simmer until it thickens.

8. Stir in chopped spinach just before removing pot from fire and add salt to taste. Serve with shredded coconut or coconut pieces.

*NOTE: If you can't get real tamarind pods, 2 teaspoons of tamarind concentrate dissolved in ¼ cup water will suffice.

MAKES 4 TO 6 SERVINGS

Spicy Coriander Tamarind Broth

Rasam

Another Jaffna Tamil specialty, this spicy, tangy, savory broth is usually sipped before a meal to prime the taste buds. It is also considered an excellent digestive. If you can't source fresh tamarind pods a ½ teaspoon of tamarind concentrate will suffice.

3 tablespoons coriander seeds
1 teaspoon white cumin seeds
1 teaspoon black peppercorns
1 head of garlic, peeled
1 dried red chili

4 cups (1 liter) water
1 tablespoon fresh tamarind, soaked
 in ¼ cup warm water with seeds
 and fiber removed
salt to taste

1. Grind the coriander seeds, cumin seeds, and peppercorns with garlic and red chili in a mortar and pestle.

2. Place mixture in a saucepan with water and tamarind and bring to a boil. Add salt to taste.

3. Remove from heat, strain, and serve.

MAKES 4 SERVINGS

Lentil Soup

Red lentils, popularly used to make *dal* in Sri Lanka, are the star of this tasty, protein-packed soup, which makes for a light evening meal or a starter.

8 ounces (250 g) red lentils
2 tablespoons oil
1 small onion, diced
2 cloves garlic, minced
2-inch (5 cm) piece ginger, minced
1 sprig curry leaves
1 tomato, peeled and chopped

1 teaspoon raw curry powder
¼ teaspoon turmeric powder
¼ teaspoon cayenne pepper powder
4 cups (1 liter) water
1 cup (250 ml) coconut milk
salt to taste

1. Wash lentils well to remove any dirt and impurities and drain.

2. Heat oil in pan. Sauté onions, garlic, ginger, curry leaves, and tomato until onions are translucent.

3. Add curry powder, turmeric powder, cayenne pepper powder, lentils, and water and bring to a boil. Reduce heat and simmer until lentils are fully cooked, about 20 minutes.

4. Add coconut milk and salt. Simmer for an additional 5 minutes.

MAKES 4 SERVINGS

Buying, Cracking & Milking a Coconut

While the coconut is still not a standard item in most grocery stores in the west, you should be able to find one at any Asian or Caribbean store. Luckily, most coconuts available here have already been stripped of their outer husk to reveal a shaggy brown sphere approximately the size of a small bowling ball.

BUYING

Select a coconut with no visible cracks or punctures. There should be no moisture leaking from the 'eyes'—three depressions located at the center of the coconut. In addition, these 'eyes' should not appear dark or moldy. Hold the coconut in your hands and shake it. It should feel heavy, and there should be some liquid sloshing around inside. No liquid indicates that the coconut is overripe and will not taste good.

CRACKING

Hold the coconut over a large bowl to catch the water that will come out. Find the seam that runs between the 'eyes' of the coconut. Using the blunt end of a heavy cleaver or knife, firmly tap on this seam as you slowly rotate the coconut in the palm of your hand. If done correctly, the coconut will split into two exact halves. If it cracks, but does not open fully, drain all the water into the bowl first. Then place the coconut on a cutting board and wedge the sharp end of the knife into the crack and pound on the cutting board to crack the coconut in half. The coconut 'meat' should be nice and white. If it has started to yellow that means the coconut is probably rancid.

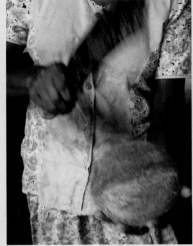

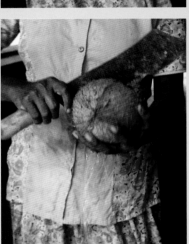

STORING

A whole coconut may be stored in the fridge for up to 2 months. The white coconut 'meat,' however, will only keep for a few days in the fridge. If you grate the meat and freeze it, it will last for 8-10 months.

Making Coconut Milk

1. Preheat your oven to 400 F for 15 minutes. Place both halves of the cracked coconut inside oven and bake for no more than 10 minutes.

2. Remove coconut halves and allow to cool. Once cool, separate the white 'meat' from the shell with a knife. Peel off any brown skin on the shell side. Break the coconut into smaller pieces and shred in a food processor.

3. Transfer the shredded coconut to a large bowl and add 2 cups of boiling water. Steep for 10 minutes and then strain through a fine mesh strainer into another bowl. Gather the remaining pulp in your hands and squeeze out all the remaining liquid, which will be the creamiest part of the extraction. Add another 2 cups of boiling water to the pulp and repeat the process.

*Nothing beats the flavor and aroma of freshly squeezed coconut milk. But if you don't want to go through all the trouble, canned coconut milk is readily available these days at most grocery stores.

Coconut Milk Gravy
Kiri Hodhi

This golden-colored gravy, infused with turmeric, comprises the base for many vegetable curries. It also serves as a light but flavorful sauce typically poured over string hoppers or *pittu* (see Rice & Breads). The lemongrass bulb is located at the root end and contains the most flavor. Smashing it with the blunt end of a knife releases its essential oils.

1 onion, sliced
2 green chilies, sliced
1 sprig curry leaves
2-inch (5 cm) section lemongrass bulb, smashed
2-inch (5 cm) cinnamon stick
2-inch (5 cm) piece pandan leaf (optional)

½ teaspoon fenugreek seeds
¼ teaspoon turmeric powder
½ cup (125 ml) water
1½ cups (375 ml) coconut milk (see previous page)
juice of one lime
salt to taste

1. Combine all ingredients (except coconut milk, lime juice and salt) in a pan. Bring to a boil.

2. Reduce to a simmer. Add coconut milk and stir well. Cook for another 5 minutes.

3. Remove from heat and cool slightly. Add a squeeze of lime juice and salt to taste.

MAKES 4 TO 6 SERVINGS

RICE & BREADS

As the staple food of Sri Lanka and, in fact, most of Asia, rice is the centerpiece of any meal, while curries are considered mere accompaniments or "rice pullers," as the locals say. Over twenty different kinds of rice are grown in Sri Lanka, the most popular for everyday use being a short-grain variety called *samba*. Akin to brown rice, red rice is also a popular option, while basmati, a fragrant, long-grain variety, is usually reserved for special occasions.

Breads, though not as popular in Sri Lanka as they are in India, offer an alternative to rice, and are usually eaten with breakfast or the evening meal.

Sri Lankan Basic Rice

This simple preparation, taught to me by my mother, will never fail to produce perfect, fluffy rice every time—even if you don't own a rice cooker. The science behind washing rice well (my lucky number is seven times) is to remove any dirt or stones as well as excess starch, which causes the rice to clump. One cup of dry rice makes about three servings, so you may scale up accordingly.

2 cups (500 g) basmati rice
2 tablespoons oil (for more flavor use butter or ghee)
1 medium onion, diced
1 sprig curry leaves
2 cardamom pods
2 cloves
2-inch (5 cm) piece pandan leaf (optional)

2-inch (5 cm) stick cinnamon
1 teaspoon salt or 1 cube chicken bouillon
2 ounces (50 g) toasted cashews for garnish (optional)
2 ounces (50 g) raisins for garnish (optional)

1. Place rice in pot and wash several times until water is mostly clear. Drain, remove from pot, and set aside.

2. Heat oil in same pot. Add onions, curry leaves, cardamom pods, cloves, pandan leaf, and cinnamon stick and fry until onions are translucent. Add rice back to pot, stir-frying for 2 to 3 minutes to remove any excess moisture and coat rice.

3. Stir in enough water to reach approximately one-inch higher than the rice. (To gauge, stick your index finger in the pot until it touches the surface of the rice. The water should reach to your first finger joint.)* Add salt or bouillon and stir until dissolved. Bring to a boil. Reduce heat to lowest setting, cover, and simmer for 15 minutes.

4. Turn off heat but leave covered for an additional 5 minutes. Then remove cover and fluff rice with a fork.

5. In a small skillet, sauté cashews and raisins in some oil and sprinkle over rice for garnish.

*NOTE: If making brown or red rice, add 1¾ cup (65 ml) water per cup of rice and increase cooking time to 45 minutes.

MAKES 6 TO 8 SERVINGS

Ghee Rice
Ghee Thel Bath

Ghee, or clarified butter, helps create the rich flavor of this rice dish. Lamb stock and ingredients such as lemongrass up the ante on flavor as well.

2 cups (500 g) basmati rice
3 tablespoons ghee
1 onion, chopped
1 sprig curry leaves
1 teaspoon coriander powder
2-inch (5 cm) stalk lemongrass
2-inch (5 cm) cinnamon stick
4 cardamom pods
4 cloves

4 peppercorns
2½ cups (625 ml) lamb stock
½ cup (125 ml) water
½ cup (125 ml) yogurt
1½ teaspoons salt
2 ounces (50 g) chopped cashew
  nuts (optional)
1 ounce (50 g) raisins (optional)

1. Wash and drain rice. Set aside.

2. Heat ghee in medium pot. Fry onions, curry leaves, coriander powder, lemongrass, cinnamon stick, cardamom pods, cloves, and peppercorns until onions are translucent. Add rice and toss for another 2 to 3 minutes. (Remove mixture to rice cooker at this point if using.)

3. Stir in stock, water, yogurt, and salt and cook until liquid evaporates, about 15 minutes.

4. Turn off heat but leave covered for an additional 5 minutes. Then remove cover, fluff rice with a fork, and stir well.

5. In a small skillet fry the cashew nuts and raisins in a small amount of oil and use to garnish the rice.

MAKES 6 TO 8 SERVINGS

Yellow Rice
Kaha Bath

This fragrant rice gets its color from turmeric and its deep flavor from the chicken stock and spices. It is usually served on more festive occasions in Sri Lanka, but go ahead, celebrate life!

2 cups (500 g) basmati rice
2 tablespoons butter or ghee
1 onion, chopped
1 sprig curry leaves
4 cardamom pods
4 cloves
1 teaspoon turmeric powder

2-inch (5 cm) stalk lemongrass
2-inch (5 cm) cinnamon stick
2-inch (5 cm) piece pandan leaf
 (optional)
2 teaspoons salt
2½ cups (625 ml) chicken stock
1 cup (250 ml) water

1. Wash and drain rice. Set aside.

2. Heat butter or ghee in a medium pot. Fry onions until translucent. Add rice, curry leaves, and all other ingredients except the stock and water. Stir-fry for 2 minutes. (Remove mixture to rice cooker at this point if using.)

3. Pour in stock and water and bring to a boil. Reduce heat, cover, and simmer until liquid evaporates, about 15 minutes.

4. Turn off heat but leave covered for an additional 5 minutes. Then remove cover and fluff rice with a fork. Stir well as the whole spices will emerge on top. They may be removed or kept as a garnish.

MAKES 6 TO 8

Coconut Milk Rice
Kiri Bath

This quick, easy, and delicious preparation is usually served for breakfast or special occasions such as weddings or Sri Lankan New Year. It may be accompanied by a chicken or beef curry, but also pairs well with *katta sambol, lunu miris,* or *seeni sambol* (see chapter on Chutneys, Pickles, Sambols & Salads). You may even give it the sweet treatment with some jaggery (palm sugar) on the side.

1 cup (250 g) short-grain rice
  (preferably jasmine)
1 cup (375 ml) water

1-inch piece pandan leaf (optional)
1 can (500 ml) coconut milk
1 teaspoon salt

1. Wash rice well and drain. Place in a pot with the water and pandan leaf (if using).

2. Bring to a boil, then reduce heat and cover and simmer for 15 minutes until most liquid has been absorbed.

3. Stir to make sure rice hasn't stuck to the bottom of the pot. Add coconut milk and salt and cook for an additional 10 minutes on lowest heat while stirring. Once rice has achieved the consistency of oatmeal, take pot off heat and cool for 2 minutes.

4. Spoon rice onto a plate and flatten to a disc-shape about 1 to 2 inches thick. Allow to set before cutting into diamond-shaped slices to serve.

MAKES 4 TO 6 SERVINGS

Vegetable Fried Rice
Elolu Bath

Whenever my mother couldn't get us to eat our vegetables, she would chop them up small and serve them in this Sri Lankan version of fried rice. I guess what makes it Sri Lankan is the addition of curry leaves and green chilies.

2 tablespoons oil
1 onion, chopped
2 cloves garlic, minced
2-inch (5 cm) piece ginger, minced
1 green chili, chopped
1 sprig curry leaves
1 spring onion, sliced

1 leek, cleaned, halved lengthwise and sliced
1 carrot, grated
1 stalk celery, chopped
2 beaten eggs (with salt and pepper)
6 cups cooked rice (any kind)
Soy sauce to taste

1. Heat 1 tablespoon oil in a fry pan or wok. Fry onions, garlic, ginger, chili, and curry leaves until onions are translucent. Add spring onions, leeks, carrot, and celery and stir-fry until soft, about 2 to 3 minutes. Move mixture to one side of the pan.

2. Add remaining 1 tablespoon oil to bare side of pan and heat for 30 seconds. Add eggs and scramble till cooked and then incorporate with vegetables and mix well. Add cooked rice and soy sauce and stir-fry for an additional 2 to 3 minutes. Serve immediately.

MAKES 6 TO 8 SERVINGS

Chicken Biriyani

Originally a dish from the royal court of the Mughals (Moguls) who once ruled the area that is now Pakistan, biriyani has become an iconic dish across South Asia and the Middle East. A staple at Sri Lankan weddings, this Muslim favorite is a serious production, made in large vats. It usually comes served with a hard-boiled egg, mint *sambol* (page 202) and *raita* (a yogurt and cucumber dressing). This home version has been scaled down to serve four people.

CHICKEN:
2 pounds (1 kg) chicken parts
2 teaspoons salt
1 teaspoon ground black pepper
1 teaspoon roasted curry powder
1 teaspoon cayenne pepper powder
  or paprika
¼ cup (65 ml) plain yogurt
¼ cup (65 ml) tomato puree
2 tablespoons chopped cashews
2 tablespoons desiccated coconut
2 cardamom pods
2 cloves
2 bay leaves
2 tablespoons ghee

1 onion, chopped
2 Serrano chilies, chopped

RICE:
1 pound (454 g) basmati rice
3 tablespoons ghee
1 onion, chopped
4 cardamom pods
4 cloves
2 bay leaves
1-inch (2.5 cm) cinnamon stick
pinch of saffron
1½ to 2 cups (375 to 500 ml) chicken
  stock
1½ teaspoons salt

1. Wash and dry chicken. Place in a large bowl and season with salt, black pepper, curry powder, and cayenne.

2. In a food processor, blend yogurt, tomato puree, cashews, and coconut. Combine blended ingredients with cardamom pods, cloves, and bay leaves and add to chicken. Toss to coat, and marinate for 30 minutes.

3. **MEANWHILE PREPARE RICE:** Wash and drain rice. Heat ghee in pan. Fry onions until translucent. Add cardamom pods, cloves, bay leaves, and cinnamon stick. Add rice and fry for a few minutes until rice starts to crackle. Add salt and pinch of saffron to stock and mix well. Pour in stock and cook covered until rice is partially cooked, about 10 minutes. Set aside.

CONTINUED

4. Heat oven to 300 degrees F (150 degrees C). Heat ghee in a pan. Fry onions and chilies until onions are translucent. Remove chicken from marinade (reserving marinade), add to pan and stir-fry for 5 to 10 minutes.

5. Add a little water to marinade and pour over chicken. Simmer for 15 to 20 minutes. Place chicken pieces in casserole dish. Place rice on top of chicken in casserole dish. Cover with aluminum foil and bake in oven until moisture evaporates, about 25 to 30 minutes.

MAKES 6 TO 8 SERVINGS

Lamb Biriyani

The classic version of biriyani is made with lamb or goat.

1½ pounds (680 g) basmati rice
1 pound (454 g) lamb or goat pieces
  (preferably, bone-in)
¼ cup (75 g) plain yogurt
2 teaspoons salt
3 teaspoons cumin powder
3 tablespoons ghee
2 onions, chopped

4 cloves garlic, sliced
1-inch (2.5 cm) piece ginger, minced
6 cardamom pods
6 cloves
2-inch (5 cm) cinnamon stick
2 bay leaves
pinch of saffron

1. Wash and soak rice for 15 minutes. Drain and set aside.

2. Cut meat into cubes and marinate in yogurt, salt, and cumin for at least 30 minutes.

3. Heat ghee in a medium pot. When hot, fry onions, garlic, ginger, cardamom pods, cloves, cinnamon stick, and bay leaves until onions are translucent.

4. Add meat and brown. Add rice and stir-fry for 2 to 3 minutes until it begins to crackle.

5. Pour in enough water to cover contents of pot plus 1 inch. Add saffron and stir. Cover and simmer for about 20 minutes until rice is tender and all liquid is absorbed.

MAKES 6 SERVINGS

Shrimp Biriyani

Reserved more for special occasions, shrimp biriyani is not very common in Sri Lanka, but offers a non-meat version of this dish. Use jumbo shrimp, keeping the heads and tails on for a more dramatic presentation.

SHRIMP:
1 pound (454 g) shrimp with shells, heads, and tails
¼ cup (65 ml) plain yogurt
4 cloves garlic, minced
2-inch (5 cm) piece ginger, minced
10 to 12 cashew nuts, ground
8 cardamom pods
2 teaspoons cayenne pepper powder
¼ teaspoon turmeric powder
1½ teaspoons roasted curry powder
1 teaspoon salt
2 tablespoons ghee
1 onion, chopped
1 sprig curry leaves
2-inch (5 cm) cinnamon stick
2-inch (5 cm) piece pandan leaf
(optional)
3 small tomatoes, blanched and diced

RICE:
1 pound (454 g) basmati rice
2 tablespoons ghee
1 onion, sliced
1 sprig curry leaves
4 cardamom pods
4 cloves
2-inch (5-cm) piece pandan leaf (optional)
2-inch (5-cm) cinnamon stick
2 cups (500 ml) water
salt to taste

1. Wash and drain shrimp leaving heads, tails, and shells intact.

2. Combine yogurt, garlic, ginger, cashews, cardamom pods, cayenne, turmeric, curry powder, and salt. Add shrimp and marinate for 20 to 30 minutes.

3. Heat ghee in a pan and fry onions until translucent. Add curry leaves, cinnamon stick, and pandan leaf. Add shrimp mixture and tomatoes and stir-fry for 3 to 4 minutes. Set aside. Heat oven to 300 degrees F (150 degrees C).

4. **PREPARE RICE:** Wash and drain rice. Heat ghee in medium pot and fry onions, curry leaves, and spices until onions are translucent. Add rice and stir-fry for 2 minutes. Add water to cover the rice plus 1-inch. Bring to a boil, cover and simmer until half-cooked, about 10 minutes (there will still be some water left).

5. When rice is half cooked, remove to a casserole dish (9x13x3). Add shrimp mixture and stir to combine. Cover with aluminum foil and cook in oven for about 15 to 20 minutes.

MAKES 6 SERVINGS

South Indian Specialties

HOPPERS, STRING HOPPERS & PITTU

Due to its proximity to India, it comes as no surprise that Sri Lankan cuisine bears the unmistakable influence of its northern neighbor. In fact, some of the most popular rice alternatives in Sri Lanka today—hoppers, string hoppers, and *pittu*—trace their origins to the south Indian states of Kerala and Tamil Nadu, which also boast some of the spiciest food on the planet. To accompany all those fiery curries, these three south Indian specialties fit the bill deliciously.

HOPPERS

The term "hoppers" is the English corruption of the Tamil word *appam*, a generic term for bread. Made from fermented rice flour and cooked in a tiny wok-shaped pan called an *appathachchi*, these crepe-like, sourdough pancakes are crispy around the edges and moist in the middle. They are usually eaten for breakfast or dinner with a meat or fish curry, some *lunu miris*, or coconut *sambol*. As deceptively simple as the batter is to prepare, they take a lot of practice to get right (as well as a well-seasoned hopper pan), so, rarely anyone makes them at home anymore. But hoppers are readily available and cheap at small street stalls or *kades* in Sri Lanka.

STRING HOPPER PRESS

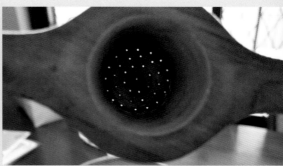

STRING HOPPERS

Delicate, steamed rice noodles or string hoppers (*idiyappam* in Tamil), on the other hand, are very labor intensive to make so they are generally bought at the same *kades*. First rice flour must be steamed; then combined with salt and water to make a soft dough. After feeding this

dough through a hand press, fine noodles are then squeezed out the other end in a circular pattern. After being placed on coaster-size bamboo mats, they are stacked on top of each other and steamed. The resulting moist, airy 'strings' are typically doused with a mild coconut milk gravy and eaten with various curries.

PITTU

Another popular rice substitute, made with rice flour and shredded coconut, is *pittu*, which is similarly labor intensive. This time the rice flour must be roasted before being combined with shredded coconut. This granular mixture is then stuffed into bamboo tubes and steamed, forming its signature cylindrical shape. While getting the right consistency is tricky, a good *pittu* crumbles easily and soaks up gravy like a sponge.

Of course, all kinds of Indian foods are popular in Sri Lanka—from Bombay sweets to rich biriyanis to savory idlis, the disk-shaped cakes made from fermented black lentils. But hoppers, string hoppers, and *pittu* have so firmly entrenched themselves into the culture of Sri Lankan cuisine that we have made them our own.

Hoppers
Appam

These fermented rice and coconut milk pancakes, originally from South India, where they are known as *appa* or *appam*, are popular for both breakfast and dinner in Sri Lanka, and available at ubiquitous roadside stands. To properly execute this dish at home, however, you will need an *appathatchchi*, a small, aluminum pan resembling a tiny wok. The thin batter is swirled around the sides, acquiring a lacy texture as it cooks while remaining soft and fluffy in the center. Sometimes a whole egg is cracked in the middle and slowly steamed with the lid on to make egg hoppers. Accompaniments include curries with gravy and Onion Chili Sambol (*Lunu Miris*; page 202) or Sugar Sambol (*Seeni Sambol*; page 197).

1 teaspoon dry yeast
1 teaspoon sugar
¼ cup (65 ml) lukewarm water
1 pound (454 g) rice flour
1 teaspoon salt

¼ teaspoon baking soda
3 tablespoons cooked rice
1 can coconut milk
3 tablespoons oil

1. Dissolve yeast and sugar in lukewarm water and set aside for 10 minutes until frothy.

2. Sift flour into bowl with salt and baking soda.

3. Place yeast mixture and flour mixture in a blender and add the cooked rice, coconut milk, and about 2 cups of warm water and blend until smooth. (The batter should be thin, but you can add more water if it isn't.) Cover with cloth and set aside on the counter to ferment for at least 6 hours.

4. When ready to make the hoppers, add a little oil to a hopper pan and heat over medium heat. Pour in about ⅓ cup of batter and rotate pan so whole surface is covered. Cook until hopper is crispy along the edges. Repeat until all the batter is cooked, oiling the pan before making each hopper. Serve immediately.

VARIATION: EGG HOPPER — After pouring batter into pan, break an egg in the center and cover and cook until done.

MAKES 10 TO 15 HOPPERS

Coconut Flat Bread
Pol Roti

As one of the few breads of Sri Lankan origin, this delicious alternative to rice may be eaten for breakfast or dinner, usually accompanied by *lunu miris* (page xx) or a meat or fish curry; or simply buttered with a banana. I find it works best with either fresh or frozen shredded coconut because of the added moisture.

1 cup (120 g) all-purpose flour
1½ cups (150 g) shredded coconut
  (fresh, frozen, or desiccated)
1 medium onion, chopped
salt to taste
2 tablespoons oil

OPTIONAL:
a few curry leaves, chopped
2 to 3 green chilies, minced
½ tablespoon Maldive fish flakes

1. Mix flour, shredded coconut, onion, and salt (as well as optional ingredients if using) together in a bowl to make a thick but pliable dough. Add a little water if necessary. Knead dough well, form into a ball, and set aside, covered, for 30 minutes.

2. Form lime-size rounds of dough and flatten to about 4 to 5 inches in diameter and about ¼ inch thick.

3. Coat pan with a little oil and cook the *roti* on each side for 4 to 5 minutes until slightly browned.

MAKES 4 TO 6 *ROTIS*

Gothamba Flat Bread
Basic Roti

This simple flatbread, similar to a flour tortilla, is probably one of the more popular varieties found in Sri Lanka. You can see men at streetside stalls expertly prepare them, flipping and twirling the dough as if making a pizza. In addition to stuffing the roti with various meat, fish, or veggie fillings, it may also be cut into thin strips and mixed with curry, vegetables, eggs, and gravy for the popular street food known as *"kottu roti"* (page 72).

1 cup (120 g) all-purpose flour
1 teaspoon salt
1 cup water

1 cup coconut oil (at room temperature)

1. In a large bowl combine flour and salt. Slowly add water and mix to form a firm dough. Add more flour if the dough is too sticky.

2. Turn dough onto a floured surface and knead a few times to create a smooth ball. Divide the ball into 8 equal-size dough balls. Place on a quarter-sheet pan and pour oil over. Make sure each of the dough balls is fully coated with oil and allow to rest for at least 30 minutes.

3. To roll the dough, place each ball on a clean surface and using your fingers, flatten it into a thin rectangle about 5x6 inches. Fold the top and bottom towards the center and then fold in the sides and press it into a rectangle again. It should be thin enough to almost see through. Place on a plate and cover with parchment or wax paper and repeat with the remaining dough balls.

4. To cook the *roti*, heat a griddle or small pan over medium heat. (No oil is necessary as the rotis have soaked up enough as they rested.)

5. Cook each roti for 1 to 2 minutes until brown patches appear and flip over and repeat on the other side. The *rotis* should be soft and pliable, not crispy. Serve immediately or store for later to make kottu.

VARIATION: EGG GOTHAMBA — As one side of the roti cooks, crack an egg in the center. Then fold over the edges and flip until the other side is fully cooked.

MAKES 8 *ROTIS*

Chapati

Chapatis have become a ubiquitous street food because they are cheap and easy to make. These South Indian flat breads have become popular in Sri Lanka as an alternative to rice and are conveniently available at numerous street stalls. But if you're not lucky enough to have one near you, they are not difficult to make.

8 ounces (250 g) all-purpose flour
salt to taste
water
oil

1. Sift the flour into a bowl and add salt. Mix in a little cold water and work until mixture forms a firm dough. Knead the dough and form into one big ball. Cover with damp cloth and set aside for 1 hour.

2. Make lime-sized balls out of the dough. Flatten by hand into discs about ⅛-inch (3mm) to ¼-inch (6mm) thick and 5-inch (13 cm) diameter.

3. Cook both sides on a hot, oiled griddle.

MAKES 4 CHAPATIS

MASALA DOSAI

Dosai

These South Indian savory pancakes provide the perfect utensil to mop up various curries or gravies. You can source ingredients like *undu* flour, which is made from black gram, at any Indian store. Dosais may be filled (usually with a potato masala curry) or made very thin for dipping (as in ghee paper dosai).

1 teaspoon sugar
1 teaspoon instant yeast
8 ounces (250 g) *undu* flour
8 ounces (250 g) all-purpose flour
1 cup (240 ml) coconut milk

FOR TEMPERING:
1 onion, chopped
3 to 4 dried red chilies, chopped
1 sprig curry leaves
½ teaspoon fenugreek seeds
½ teaspoon black mustard seeds
2 tablespoons oil

1. Soak sugar and yeast in a little lukewarm water for 10 minutes until frothy.

2. Mix *undu* and all-purpose flours with yeast mixture. Cover and set aside. When mixture doubles in size, add coconut milk. The resulting batter should be of pouring consistency.

3. Fry the tempering ingredients together in the oil in a small pan and add to batter.

4. Heat an 8-inch skillet or griddle and brush with a little oil. Use about ⅓ cup (80 ml) of batter per *dosai* and spread uniformly across pan. When small bubbles start appearing flip pancake and cook other side for 1 to 2 minutes. Remove to a plate.

MAKES 8 *DOSAI*

GHEE PAPER DOSAI

MEAT & POULTRY

Despite the predominantly Buddhist and Hindu population, who are mostly vegetarian, meat inevitably appears on the daily table in Sri Lanka. Chicken is the standout favorite with pork and wild boar being less popular. But Muslims, who eschew pork, enjoy beef and mutton (goat).

NOTE: When making many of the curries I give you the option at the end of adding 1 cup of coconut milk or a little tomato paste. By adding the coconut milk you get a lighter-colored curry with the flavor of coconut, while the tomato paste gives you a darker curry with more complex flavors.

Chicken Curry
Kukul Mas Curry

A mainstay of Sri Lankan cuisine, this dish was the first curry I learned to make. Like any curry, its flavor is greatly enhanced the longer it has been marinating—both before and after cooking. That's why this dish always tastes better the next day. The last two ingredients, tomato paste and coconut milk, are typically used to thicken the gravy, so only use one of them.

1 whole fryer chicken, cut into individual pieces, or use parts
3 tablespoons roasted curry powder
1 to 2 teaspoons cayenne pepper powder
1 teaspoon turmeric powder
1 teaspoon apple cider vinegar
1 teaspoon salt
2 tablespoons oil
1 large onion, sliced

4 cloves garlic, sliced
2-inch (5 cm) piece ginger, chopped
1 sprig curry leaves
2-inch (5 cm) stalk lemongrass
3 cardamom pods
3 cloves
1-inch (2.5 cm) cinnamon stick
2 teaspoons tomato paste; or 1 cup (250 ml) coconut milk (optional)

1. Wash and clean chicken, removing most fat. Place chicken in bowl with curry powder, cayenne pepper powder, turmeric, vinegar, and salt. Mix well with hands to coat chicken and set aside for at least 30 minutes. (**NOTE**: Marinate the chicken overnight for optimum results.)

2. In a large pot, heat oil. Once hot, add onions, garlic, ginger, curry leaves, lemongrass, cardamom pods, cloves, and cinnamon stick. Fry until onions are translucent.

3. Add chicken pieces (reserving any leftover marinade in bowl) and cook, stirring occasionally until chicken is browned.

4. Fill the marinade bowl with water and slosh around to catch any remaining marinade and add to pot. The chicken should be fully immersed. Bring to a boil. Then reduce heat, cover, and simmer for about 25 minutes.

5. Stir in tomato paste or coconut milk (see Note, page 107) and simmer, uncovered, for an additional 10 minutes.

MAKES 6 SERVINGS

Pork Curry
Ooroomas Curry

The key to pork curry, according to my late Aunty Dora, is to cut the pork into thick chunks and leave all the fat on. "That's where the flavor is," she says. Tamarind also adds a nice tangy note to cut the overall spiciness of this dish.

1 tablespoon fresh tamarind, or
  1 teaspoon tamarind concentrate
4 tablespoons roasted curry powder
2 pounds (1 kg) boneless pork, cut
  into 1-inch cubes
2 teaspoons cayenne pepper powder
2 teaspoons salt
2 tablespoons oil
1 large onion, chopped

4 cloves garlic, chopped
2-inch (5 cm) piece ginger, ground
2-inch (5 cm) cinnamon stick
2-inch (5 cm) stalk lemongrass
2 green chilies, sliced
1 sprig curry leaves
1½ cups (375 ml) water
½ cup (125 ml) coconut milk,
  or 1 tablespoon tomato paste

1. Soak fresh tamarind in a little warm water; strain and remove seeds and fiber. (If using concentrate stir into a little warm water.) Slightly roast curry powder in a pan for 2 to 3 minutes.

2. Place pork in a bowl with tamarind water, roasted curry powder, cayenne pepper powder, and salt, and marinate for 30 minutes.

3. Heat oil in a pan. When hot, fry onions, garlic, ginger, cinnamon stick, lemongrass, green chilies, and curry leaves until onions are translucent.

4. Add pork (reserving any marinade left in bowl) and stir-fry until browned. Fill the marinade bowl with the water and slosh around to catch any remaining marinade and pour into pan to cover pork. Bring to a boil. Reduce heat, cover, and simmer until pork is tender (about 25 to 30 minutes).

5. Add coconut milk or tomato paste (see Note, page 107) and simmer, uncovered, another 10 minutes or until gravy is thick.

MAKES 6 TO 8 SERVINGS

Beef Curry
Harak Mas Curry

As the majority of Sri Lankans are either Buddhist or Hindu, beef is not a popular option on the island. As a result, the quality of their beef is not quite up to western standards. But that shouldn't prevent you from enjoying this dish. Unlike pork curry, cutting the beef into smaller cubes allows the meat to better tenderize while slow cooking in its rich gravy.

4 tablespoons curry powder
½ teaspoon fenugreek
2 pounds (1 kg) beef, cut into 1-inch (2.5-cm) cubes
1 to 2 teaspoons cayenne pepper powder
1 teaspoon paprika
2 teaspoons apple cider vinegar
2 teaspoons salt
2 tablespoons oil
1 large onion, chopped

4 cloves garlic, sliced
2-inch (5 cm) piece ginger, minced
2 green chilies, sliced
1 sprig curry leaves
2-inch (5 cm) stalk lemongrass
2-inch (5 cm) cinnamon stick
2 cardamom pods
1 clove
1 cup (250 ml) water
1 cup (250 ml) coconut milk; or 1 tablespoon tomato paste

1. Slightly toast curry powder and fenugreek in a pan. Mix with beef and add cayenne pepper powder, paprika, vinegar, and salt and marinate for 1 to 2 hours (or overnight, for optimum results).

2. Heat oil in pan. Sauté onions, garlic, ginger, green chilies, curry leaves, lemongrass, cinnamon stick, cardamom pods, and cloves until onions are translucent.

3. Add beef and stir-fry for several minutes until beef is browned. Slosh a little water in marinade bowl to release the remaining spice mixture and add to pan. Add remaining water and bring to a boil. Reduce heat, cover, and simmer for 30 minutes.

4. Add coconut milk or tomato paste (see Note, page 107) and simmer, uncovered, for an additional 20 minutes until gravy is thick.

MAKES 6 TO 8 SERVINGS

Lamb/Mutton Curry
Elu Mas Curry

This dish can be made with either lamb or goat (mutton), which is a popular alternative to beef in Sri Lanka.

2 pounds (1 kg) lamb or mutton, cut into 1-inch (2.5-cm) cubes
3 tablespoons roasted curry powder
1 to 2 teaspoons cayenne pepper powder
1 tablespoon apple cider vinegar
2 teaspoons salt
2 tablespoons oil
1 large onion, diced

4 cloves garlic, minced
2-inch (5 cm) piece ginger, minced
2 green chilies, sliced
2-inch (5 cm) stalk lemongrass
2-inch (5 cm) cinnamon stick
1 sprig curry leaves
1 cup (375 ml) water
1 cup (375 ml) coconut milk; or 1 tablespoon tomato paste

1. Prick meat all over with a fork to tenderize. Slightly toast curry powder in a pan for 2 to 3 minutes. Mix with meat and add cayenne pepper powder, vinegar, and salt and marinate for 1 to 2 hours (or overnight for optimum results).

2. Heat oil in pan. Sauté onions, garlic, ginger, green chilies, lemongrass, cinnamon stick, and curry leaves until onions are translucent.

3. Add marinated meat and stir-fry for a few minutes until browned. Add the water and bring to boil. Reduce heat, cover, and simmer for 30 minutes.

4. Add coconut milk or tomato paste (see Note, page 107) and simmer, uncovered, for an additional 20 minutes on low heat.

MAKES 6 SERVINGS

Jaffna Goat Curry

Since the largely Hindu Tamils don't eat beef, goat offers a good alternative. This version of goat curry kicks up the heat a few notches due to the Jaffna curry powder and added dry chilies.

1 pound (454 g) goat meat
  (preferably bone-in), cut into
  1-inch (2.5-cm) pieces
2 tablespoons Jaffna curry powder
1 teaspoon salt
2 tablespoons oil
1 onion, diced

2 dry red chilies, broken up
1 sprig curry leaves
½ teaspoon fennel seeds
½ teaspoon black mustard seeds
1 cup (250 ml) water
1 cup (250 ml) coconut milk; or
  1 tablespoon tomato paste

1. Season goat meat with curry powder and salt and set aside.

2. Heat oil in pan. Sauté onions, chilies, and curry leaves until onions are translucent. Add fennel seeds and mustard seeds and sauté another minute.

3. Add the seasoned goat meat and stir-fry for 2 minutes until meat is browned. Add the water and bring to a boil. Cover, reduce heat and simmer for 30 minutes.

4. Add coconut milk or tomato paste (see Note, page 107) and salt to taste and simmer, uncovered, an additional 30 minutes until meat is tender and gravy is thick.

MAKES 4 TO 6 SERVINGS

Chicken Liver, Pea & Cashew Curry

This unique combination is often served as an accompaniment to biriyani.

¼ pound (125 g) raw cashew nuts
½ pound (225 g) chicken livers
2 teaspoons coriander powder
½ teaspoon cumin powder
1 teaspoon cayenne pepper powder
½ teaspoon ground black pepper
½ teaspoon apple cider vinegar
2 tablespoons oil

1 onion, sliced
2 cloves garlic, sliced
2 cardamom pods
1-inch (1.25 cm) cinnamon stick
1 sprig curry leaves
¼ pound (125 g) frozen peas
1 cup (250 ml) coconut milk
1¼ teaspoons salt

1. Soak cashews in water for 2 to 3 hours. Drain and set aside.

2. Wash chicken livers and remove any membrane and discolored parts. Place in bowl and add coriander, cumin, cayenne pepper powder, black pepper and vinegar and marinate for at least 30 minutes.

3. Heat oil in pan. Sauté onions, garlic, cardamom pods, cinnamon stick, and curry leaves until onions are translucent. Add marinated chicken livers and stir-fry for 5 minutes. Remove livers.

4. Add cashews, peas, coconut milk, and salt and simmer for 20 minutes. Add fried chicken livers and cook an additional 5 minutes.

MAKES 4 TO 6 SERVINGS

Egg Curry

This very mild dish is often a young child's first curry.

4 hard-boiled eggs
¼ teaspoon turmeric powder
2 tablespoons oil
1 onion, chopped
3 cloves garlic, minced
1-inch piece ginger, sliced
2 green chilies, slit from base to
  stem
1-inch piece pandan leaf (optional)

1-inch stalk lemongrass
1-inch cinnamon stick
2 teaspoons raw curry powder
1 sprig curry leaves
1 cup (250 ml) coconut milk
pinch of saffron
salt to taste
juice of one lime

1. Shell eggs and prick them with toothpick in 2 or 3 places so they don't burst while frying. Rub eggs with turmeric powder. Heat oil in frying pan. Fry eggs until golden brown on outside. Remove and set aside.

2. Fry onions, garlic, ginger, green chilies, pandan leaf, lemongrass, cinnamon stick, curry powder, and curry leaves until onions are translucent.

3. Add coconut milk and saffron and almost bring to a boil. Add salt to taste. Then reduce heat and simmer for 10 to 15 minutes.

4. Add fried hardboiled eggs and cook for an additional 5 minutes.

5. Cool slightly and squeeze on lime juice. Mix well before serving.

MAKES 4 SERVINGS

Duck Curry with Arrack
Thara Curry

Though duck is not very popular in Sri Lanka, this dish is a throwback to the Dutch colonial era. Arrack, the liquor of choice in Sri Lanka, is distilled from the sap of the coconut palm flower. It perfectly cuts and complements the richness of this dish, but if you can't find any, rum or whiskey will do just fine.

2 tablespoons roasted curry powder
1 tablespoon cayenne pepper powder
½ teaspoon ground black pepper
1 whole duck, separated into parts
juice of one lime
3 tablespoons vinegar
½ teaspoon turmeric powder
1 teaspoon salt
1 onion, diced
4 cloves garlic, minced
2-inch (5 cm) piece ginger, minced
1 sprig curry leaves

2-inch (5 cm) piece pandan leaf (optional)
2-inch (5 cm) stalk lemongrass
2-inch (5 cm) cinnamon stick
½ cup (125 ml) water
1½ cups (375 ml) coconut milk
1 tablespoon sugar
¼ cup (65 ml) arrack or whiskey

FOR TEMPERING:
2 tablespoons oil or ghee
1 onion, diced
1 sprig curry leaves

1. Slightly toast curry powder, cayenne pepper powder, and black pepper.

2. Wash and cut duck into 3-inch pieces. Rub with lime juice, vinegar, turmeric powder, salt, and toasted spices. Marinate for at least 3 hours (or overnight for optimum results).

3. Place duck in a medium pot with onions, garlic, ginger, curry leaves, pandan leaf, lemongrass, cinnamon stick, water, and coconut milk. Bring to a boil, then cover, reduce heat and simmer until duck is cooked, about 30 minutes.

4. Add sugar and arrack and simmer for an additional 10 to 15 minutes. Remove duck and reserve gravy.

5. To temper, heat oil or ghee in a large skillet and fry onions and curry leaves. Add duck pieces and brown. Add gravy and stir for 2 to 3 minutes. Serve on a platter garnished with crispy fried potato sticks.

MAKES 6 SERVINGS

Aunt Padma's Beef Smore

This traditional version of pot roast, adapted from the Dutch Burghers, transformed into a uniquely Sri Lankan creation with the addition of lime pickle, chilies, coconut milk, and spices. This recipe came from my late Aunt Padma, an accomplished cook, who considered it one of her specialties even though she didn't even eat meat.

1 piece (3 to 4 pounds / 1.5 to 2 kgs) beef tenderloin
1 tablespoon lime pickle
2 tablespoons coriander powder
1 tablespoon cayenne pepper powder
½ teaspoon fenugreek seeds
2 teaspoons cumin powder, roasted
2 teaspoons fennel powder, roasted
1 onion, chopped
2 cloves garlic, minced

2-inch (5 cm) piece ginger, minced
1 sprig curry leaves
2 cloves
2-inch (5 cm) stalk lemongrass
1-inch (2.5 cm) cinnamon stick
3 tablespoons vinegar
3 cups (750 ml) water
1 cup (250 ml) coconut milk
3 tablespoons oil
1½ teaspoons salt

1. Wash and dry meat, and remove most fat and all gristle. Prick with fork all over to tenderize, or pound with meat hammer. Rub with lime pickle, coriander powder, cayenne powder, fenugreek seeds, cumin powder, and fennel powder. Marinate for at least 2 to 3 hours (or overnight for optimum results).

2. Put beef tenderloin, half the onions, the garlic, ginger, curry leaves, cloves, lemongrass, cinnamon stick, vinegar, and water into a medium pot. Bring to a boil, then reduce heat and simmer, uncovered, until meat is tender and liquid has almost evaporated, about 1½ to 2 hours.

3. Add coconut milk and simmer for an additional 10 minutes. Remove meat and reduce gravy on low heat by about a half.

4. Heat oil in a separate pan and sauté reserved onions until golden brown. Add meat and brown on all sides. Slice meat and place on a serving tray and pour gravy over the meat.

MAKES 4 TO 6 SERVINGS

Aunty Stella's Black Pork Curry

I first enjoyed this dish at my good friends' Sudath & Rushmi's house. Sudath's mother, Aunty Stella, prepared it for a dinner party, and it tasted so good, I had to see how she made it. Of course, like any good Sri Lankan home cook, she never measured any of the ingredients. So I hope I have captured the essence of what she made so you can reproduce this wonderful dish in your own kitchen.

NOTE: Since 'kalu' means black in Sinhalese, black pork curry is sometimes confused with *kalu pol pork* in Sri Lanka, but they are actually two different dishes. Black pork curry gets its name from the black pepper, *goraka (Garcinia gamboge)*, and the dark roasted curry powder used in the dish. *Kalu pol pork*, on the other hand, utilizes roasted shredded coconut, which adds a smoky flavor and helps thicken the base.

3 pounds (about 1½ kg) pork belly or pork shoulder (or ideally a combination of the two), cut into 1-inch chunks with fat intact
¼ cup tamarind water*
¼ cup coconut vinegar or apple cider vinegar
1 teaspoon salt
3 teaspoons ground black pepper
1 teaspoon turmeric powder
3 teaspoons raw curry powder
5 tablespoons roasted curry powder
2 to 3 teaspoons cayenne pepper powder
4 tablespoons coconut oil

1 large onion, diced
2 teaspoons garlic paste
2 teaspoons ginger paste
2 sprigs curry leaves
2-inch piece Pandan leaf (optional)
2 lemongrass bulbs, smashed (**NOTE:** the bulbs are located at the root end)
4 to 5 green chilies, sliced
½ teaspoon fenugreek seeds
3 pieces of *goraka* (optional)
3 cardamom pods
3 cloves
2-inch cinnamon stick
2 cups water

1. Wash pork and drain. Add tamarind water, vinegar, salt, pepper, turmeric, raw and roasted curry powders, and cayenne pepper powder and mix well. Marinate for at least one hour (or up to 4 hours).

2. Heat oil in a large pot. Add onions, garlic paste, ginger paste, curry leaves, pandan leaf, lemongrass, green chilies, fenugreek seeds, and goraka, and stir-fry until onion is translucent.

3. Roughly smash cardamom pods, cloves, and cinnamon stick in a mortar and pestle and add to pot, stirring 2 to 3 minutes until fragrant.

4. Add pork and stir to mix. Lower heat, cover, and simmer for 10 minutes. Add 2 cups of water and stir. Cook covered for 45 minutes until pork is tender.

*NOTE: To make tamarind water, soak 1 tablespoon fresh tamarind in some warm water and strain fiber and seeds; or use 1 teaspoon of tamarind concentrate soaked in ¼ cup water.

MAKES 6 TO 8 SERVINGS

Malay Spicy Beef Braise
Goreng Dajing

My good friend, Chef Mohara Dole, who offers local cooking classes through her company, Cooking by Colours, made this delightful dish for lunch one day as I watched and took notes. Though I put my own spin on the following recipe, it represents the legacy of the Sri Lankan Malay community, who were brought to Sri Lanka by the Dutch as indentured servants in the 17th century.

2 pound (1 kg) beef chuck roast, fat trimmed
2 teaspoons salt
3 teaspoons tamarind juice
3 tablespoons oil
2 medium onions, sliced
2 tablespoons minced garlic
2 tablespoons minced ginger root
2 to 4 green chilies, sliced
2 sprigs curry leaves
2-inch piece pandan leaf (optional)

2 tablespoons tomato paste
2-inch cinnamon stick
4 cardamom pods
4 cloves
½ teaspoon fenugreek seeds
1 tablespoon cayenne pepper powder
1 tablespoon raw curry powder
1 teaspoon roasted curry powder
Juice of one lime
2 tablespoons oil

1. Wash and dry beef. Cut into about 4 large chunks and rub with salt and tamarind juice and marinate for 1 to 2 hours.

2. Heat oil in a deep pot or pressure cooker. Add half of onion slices, the garlic, ginger, 2 of the green chilies, the curry leaves, pandan leaf, and tomato paste, and sauté until onions are translucent.

3. Add cinnamon stick, cardamom pods, cloves, fenugreek seeds, and dry spices. Sauté an additional 2 minutes, stirring constantly so that nothing sticks to the bottom of the pot.

4. Add marinated beef to the pot. Add enough water to cover beef, and pressure cook for 30 minutes; if using a regular pot, cook on medium to low heat for about an hour, or until meat is fork tender.

CONTINUED

5. Remove meat from pot, pat dry, and set aside on a plate. Turn heat down to low and reduce the gravy to about half.

6. Carefully smash each chunk of meat, sprinkle with salt to taste and lime juice. Heat oil in a sauté pan. When pan is hot, sear meat, 2 chunks at a time, until well-browned on the outside.

7. After gravy has been reduced, add browned meat back into the pot and simmer about 5 minutes. Garnish with raw onion slices and some additional green chilies slices.

MAKES 6 TO 8 SERVINGS

Lampreis

Lampreis has got to be one of my favorite Sri Lankan dishes. On face value, it appears to be nothing more than a bundle of rice and curry wrapped up in a banana leaf, but such simplicity belies the dish's nuance and complexity. Dating back to the Dutch colonial era, its name literally means, "parcel of rice," but I doubt you'll find anything remotely like it in Holland. The origins of *lampreis* can be traced to the island of Java in Indonesia, formerly Batavia, where the Dutch East India Company was based, therefore it is a dish most associated with the Eurasian community of Dutch Burghers.

While purists argue about what exactly constitutes *lampreis*, a consensus has emerged regarding its components, which include: short-grain samba rice cooked in a rich stock; tempered brinjal or eggplant *pahi*, a dry curry; a *frikkadel*, or meatball, which today has been replaced by a beef cutlet; a mixed meat curry of chicken, pork, and beef or mutton; *seeni sambol*; fried ash plantain; and prawn *blachan*, a condiment of Indonesian origin made of dried prawns, onions, salt, tamarind, and spices all ground together into a pungent paste. Prepared individually, these dishes are then assembled in a banana leaf, and wrapped up and steamed, so that the flavors meld together. The result is a rich and flavorful meal, miles away from the run-of-the-mill rice packets that Sri Lankans favor as a portable lunch. Whether it's the earthy flavor of the banana leaf that gives it that added umph or the interplay of the individual dishes themselves, to know *lampreis* is to love it.

In Sri Lanka today, many banana-leaf wrapped bundles masquerade as the real deal, but the best commercially available product can usually be found at either a bakery chain called The Fab, and, of course, the Dutch Burgher Union. Though the latter is a members-only club, thankfully, they sell *lampreis* at their cafe in the back. You can do even better if you are lucky enough to know one of the handful of Dutch burgher ladies who still make *lampreis* for private orders. If you are feeling ambitious, however, try making it yourself with the tried and tested recipe here.

Lampreis

A portable rice & curry meal wrapped and steamed in a banana leaf, *lampreis* is considered a single dish with seven components. The most important component is, of course, the rice, which must be prepared in a rich stock, usually of beef (though chicken stock is acceptable as well). In Sri Lanka, a short-grain variety of rice known as *suduru samba* is used, but as that may be difficult to source, I use basmati. The dish's main protein is Mixed Meat Curry—usually made with some combination of chicken, beef, pork, or mutton—in which the meats are cut into small, bite-size morsels. The only other meat in the dish is the *frikkadel*, originally a meatball, that

was gradually replaced by a Beef Cutlet. Included as well are Fried Ash Plantains, Eggplant *Pahi* (a dry curry), Sugar Sambol (*Seeni Sambola*), and Prawn *Blachan*. Once all these individual components are made, the whole dish may be assembled in a section of cut banana leaf. Since it's impossible to make a small amount of *lampreis*, this recipe will produce 10 to 12 individual packets. Though a labor intensive and ambitious undertaking, anyone sampling the final product should be duly impressed.

MIXED MEAT CURRY

½ pound boneless beef or mutton, cut into 1-inch cubes
½ pound boneless chicken, cut into 1-inch cubes
½ pound boneless pork, cut into 1-inch cubes
2 tablespoons roasted curry powder
2 teaspoons cayenne pepper powder
1 teaspoon turmeric powder
1 teaspoon ground cardamom
1 teaspoon ground cloves

½ teaspoon fenugreek seeds
1 teaspoon salt
2 tablespoons oil
1 onion, finely chopped
1 sprig curry leaves
2-inch piece pandan leaf
4 cloves garlic, minced
2-inch piece ginger, minced
1-inch stalk lemongrass
2-inch cinnamon stick

1. Wash and dry meats. In a bowl toss meats with dry spices and salt to coat and let marinate for at least 30 minutes.

2. Heat oil in pan. Add onions, curry leaves, and pandan leaf and sauté until onions are translucent. Add garlic, ginger, lemongrass, and cinnamon stick and sauté an additional 5 minutes. Add marinated meat and brown. Add enough water to cover meat and bring to a boil. Reduce heat, cover, and simmer for 40 minutes.

3. Remove lid and cook for an additional 10 minutes or until gravy thickens. Remove cinnamon stick, lemongrass stalk, and pandan leaf. Set meat aside for assembly.

RICE

4 cups basmati rice (or *suduru samba*)
2 tablespoons ghee or butter
1 onion, diced
1 sprig curry leaves
2-inch piece pandan leaf

cheesecloth
2-inch cinnamon stick
5 cardamom pods
4 cloves
6 cups beef or chicken stock
2 teaspoons salt

1. Wash rice several times to remove any impurities and starch. Drain well and set aside.

2. Heat ghee or butter in a large pot. Add onions, curry leaves, and pandan leaf and sauté until onions are translucent.

3. Add rice and sauté an additional 5 minutes, until rice is coated. Using the cheesecloth, tie up the cinnamon stick, cardamom pods, and cloves, and add to pot along with stock and salt. Stir well. The liquid should rise to a level approximately 1-inch above the rice.

4. Bring to a boil and cover. Reduce heat to lowest setting and cook for 15 minutes. Turn off heat but leave covered for an additional 10 minutes. Remove lid and fluff rice with a fork, removing spice packet.

CONTINUED

FRIED ASH PLANTAINS

Starchier green plantains, which have a milder taste, are the variety used for this dish.

3 green plantains, peeled and cut
  into 1-inch cubes
1 teaspoon cayenne pepper powder

1 teaspoon turmeric powder
1 teaspoon salt
Oil for deep-frying

1. Toss plantains with cayenne pepper powder, turmeric powder, and salt.

2. Heat oil to 350 degrees F. Fry plantains in batches until golden brown. Remove with a slotted spoon and let cool on a wire rack lined with paper towels. Set aside for assembly.

PRAWN BLACHAN

To make this paste you will need the small, dried shrimp usually available at Asian stores. Maldive fish flakes may be sourced online at a Sri Lankan grocer (but if you can't find them use the same amount of dried shrimp).

½ cup dried shrimp
2 tablespoons oil
1 medium onion, diced
2 cloves garlic, coarsely chopped
1-inch piece ginger, coarsely
  chopped
1 sprig curry leaves

5 dried red chilies, broken into
  pieces and stems removed
1 tablespoon Maldive fish flakes
1 tablespoon tamarind juice
1 tablespoon sugar
Salt to taste

1. Wash shrimp and reconstitute them in hot water for a few minutes. Pat dry and set aside.

2. Heat oil in a pan. Sauté onion, garlic, ginger, and curry leaves until onions are translucent. Add the shrimp, dried chilies, Maldive fish, tamarind juice, sugar and stir to incorporate.

3. Allow to cool slightly before removing contents of pan to a mortar & pestle or food processor. Grind to a thick paste, adding salt to taste. Set aside for assembly.

REMAINING COMPONENTS

Eggplant Pahi (To prepare, use recipe for Eggplant Curry on page 158 but omit the coconut milk.)
Beef Cutlets (see p. 57)

Sugar Sambol (*Seeni Sambola*, see p. 197)
banana leaves
twine or toothpicks

ASSEMBLY & BAKING

1. Cut 12 squares (12x12 inches) of banana leaf using sections on either side of the leaf rib. Turn on a burner of your stovetop and run each piece back and forth over the flame a couple times to make the leaf squares more pliable. Place leaf squares, shiny side down, on a flat work surface.

2. Add about 1 cup of rice to the center of one leaf. On the top edge of the rice, you can add about 2 to 3 tablespoons of the Meat Curry. Add around the rice 1 tablespoon each of the Fried Plantains, Eggplant Pahi, and Sugar Sambol, and 1 teaspoon of Prawn Blachan. Place two Beef Cutlets at the top.

3. Bring the top and bottom edges of the banana leaf towards the center so they meet. Slightly flatten the contents of the *lampreis* and fold these two edges over one another. Then fold both sides together over the center to create a rectangle. Flip over and secure with a piece of twine or toothpick. Lay the *lampreis* on a baking sheet and continue assembling the packets until all banana leaf squares are filled.

4. To serve, preheat oven to 350 degrees F. Bake for 15 to 20 minutes until hot. The assembled *lampreis* packets may be frozen or kept in the fridge for up to three days and reheated.

RICE & CURRY

FISH & SEAFOOD

As islanders, Sri Lankans enjoy the bounty of the Indian ocean as well as the lakes, rivers, and lagoons around the country. Frozen seafood is virtually unheard of as people prefer the catch of the day. While certain products such as tuna and massive lagoon crabs are earmarked for export, plenty is consumed locally as well.

Squid Curry
Dhallo Curry

Squid, or cuttlefish as they call it in Sri Lanka, needs to be cooked either very quickly or for a long time so it does not acquire a rubbery texture. This curried method is both fast and easy, yielding a delicious dish. Be sure to clean the squid thoroughly by removing its plastic-like 'spine' and ink sac and peeling off the purplish skin.

1 pound (454 g) squid
2 tablespoons roasted curry powder
1 teaspoon fenugreek seeds
1 to 2 teaspoons cayenne pepper
  powder
2 tablespoons oil
1 onion, chopped

4 cloves garlic, minced
2-inch (5 cm) piece ginger, minced
2 to 3 green chilies, sliced
1 sprig curry leaves
1½ cups (375 ml) coconut milk
salt to taste
juice of one lime

1. Wash, clean, and cut squid into 1-inch (2.5 cm) rings. Keep tentacles intact. Mix squid with curry powder, fenugreek seeds, and cayenne pepper powder. Set aside.

2. Heat oil in pan. Fry onions, garlic, ginger, green chilies, and curry leaves until onions are translucent.

3. Add squid and stir-fry for 2 to 3 minutes until opaque. Add coconut milk and salt and bring to a boil. Reduce heat and simmer for 5 minutes.

4. Cool slightly and stir in lime juice before serving.

MAKES 6 SERVINGS

Leela's Chilaw Crab Curry
Kakuluwo Curry

Leela, the sweet little lady who taught me this dish, worked as my Aunt Dora's cook for some forty plus years. Hailing from the town of Chilaw on the west coast, a place famous for their fiery crab curry, she never failed to make this for me when I visited. Since not many members of my extended family in Sri Lanka could handle food this hot, I usually ended up eating the whole dish myself (What can I say? I don't like to waste food!). Of course, for a more moderate version, take it easy on the cayenne pepper. Murunga leaves, though difficult to source, counteract the heat of the curry.

6 large blue crabs
2 tablespoons roasted curry powder
2 tablespoons cayenne pepper powder
½ teaspoon turmeric powder
¼ teaspoon allspice powder
1 teaspoon salt
1 tablespoon raw rice
½ teaspoon black peppercorns
1 teaspoon cumin seeds
3 tablespoons shredded coconut
5 cloves garlic, sliced

2 tablespoons oil
1 onion, diced
1 sprig curry leaves
1 tomato, chopped
2-inch (5 cm) piece pandan leaf (optional)
½ cup (125 ml) water
1 cup (250 ml) coconut milk
2 tablespoons fresh tamarind; or
  1 teaspoon tamarind concentrate
1 bunch murunga leaves (optional)

1. Wash and clean crabs (removing gills and dirt). Split body cavity down the middle and slightly crack legs with a nutcracker to allow gravy to penetrate. Toss crabs with curry powder, cayenne pepper powder, turmeric, allspice, and salt. Set aside.

2. In a small skillet, toast rice, peppercorns, and cumin seeds for 2 minutes. Remove to a plate and roast coconut until it turns brown. Grind all these ingredients with the garlic in a mortar and pestle or food processor and set aside.

3. Heat oil in medium pot. Sauté onions, curry leaves, tomato, and pandan leaf until onions are translucent. Add crabs and ½ cup water. Cover and steam over high heat for 10 minutes.

4. Combine coconut mixture and coconut milk and add to pot. Stir and simmer for 5 to 10 minutes until it thickens.

5. Soak tamarind in ¼ cup water. Strain seeds and fiber and add liquid to pot (or if using concentrate stir into ¼ cup water and dissolve). Simmer an additional 5 minutes. Remove from heat and stir in murunga leaves.

MAKES 4 TO 6 SERVINGS

Shrimp Curry
Isso Curry

As shrimp or prawns are plentiful on the island, this is a popular dish in Sri Lanka. It also happens to be one of my favorites because of the complexity of flavors from spicy to tangy (thanks to the addition of tamarind).

1 pound (454 g) shrimp
2 tablespoons curry powder
1 to 2 teaspoons cayenne pepper
  powder
¼ teaspoon fenugreek seeds
2 tablespoons fresh tamarind; or
  1 teaspoon tamarind concentrate
2 tablespoons oil
1 onion, sliced
1 tablespoon crushed fresh ginger

4 cloves garlic, minced
2 to 3 green chilies, sliced
1 sprig curry leaves
2-inch (2.5 cm) piece pandan leaf
  (optional)
2-inch (2.5 cm) stalk lemongrass
2-inch (2.5 cm) cinnamon stick
1 cup (250 ml) coconut milk
salt to taste
juice of one lime

1. Wash, shell, and devein shrimp.

2. Slightly roast curry powder, cayenne pepper powder, and fenugreek seeds for 2 minutes. Toss shrimp with spice mixture and set aside for 30 minutes.

3. Soak fresh tamarind in ¼ cup water and strain, reserving water and discarding seeds and fiber (or if using concentrate stir into ¼ cup water and dissolve). Set aside.

4. Heat oil in pan. Sauté onions, ginger, garlic, green chilies, curry leaves, pandan leaf, lemongrass, and cinnamon stick until onions are translucent.

5. Add seasoned shrimp and stir-fry with other ingredients for 2 minutes. Add tamarind water to pot along with coconut milk and salt. Gently simmer until shrimp turn pink. Be careful NOT TO OVERCOOK. Squeeze lime juice over shrimp before serving.

MAKES 4 TO 6 SERVINGS

Red Fish Curry
Miris Malu

As the name suggests, this dish skews to the spicier side, as red connotes chili powder (cayenne). For a less spicy version, reverse the amounts of cayenne pepper powder and paprika. I recommend using tuna steaks for this dish or whatever firm-fleshed fish you prefer.

2 pounds (1 kg) firm-fleshed fish (such as tuna steaks), cut into 1-inch chunks
1 tablespoon fresh tamarind; or ½ teaspoon tamarind concentrate
2 tablespoons roasted curry powder
1 to 2 teaspoons cayenne pepper powder
¼ teaspoon fenugreek seeds
1 teaspoon paprika

2 tablespoons oil
1 onion, sliced
2-inch (5 cm) piece ginger, sliced
3 cloves garlic, sliced
2 to 3 green chilies, slit from stem to tip
1 sprig curry leaves
1½ cups (325 ml) water
1½ teaspoons salt

1. Rinse and dry fish. Soak tamarind in ¼ cup water and strain, reserving water and discarding seeds and fiber (or if using concentrate stir into ¼ cup water and dissolve).

2. Toss fish in tamarind solution along with the curry powder, cayenne pepper powder, fenugreek seeds, and paprika and marinate for at least 30 minutes.

3. Heat oil in pan. Sauté onions, ginger, garlic, green chilies, and curry leaves until onions are translucent. Add fish to pan with water and salt. Bring to a boil and then reduce heat and simmer for 10 to 15 minutes until fish is cooked through.

MAKES 6 TO 8 SERVINGS

White Fish Curry
Malu Kirata

This curry is a much milder, coconut milk-based dish popular among children. In fact, it is one of the first curries fed to toddlers. Slitting the green chilies curbs their heat. Kingfish or mackerel work really well with this dish.

2 pounds (1 kg) white fish steaks or fillets, cut into 1-inch chunks
juice of one lime
1½ teaspoons salt
⅛ teaspoon turmeric powder
2 tablespoons oil
1 onion, sliced
3 cloves garlic, sliced

2 to 3 green chilies, slit from stem to base
1 sprig curry leaves
1 cup (250 ml) coconut milk
½ cup (125 ml) water
2-inch (5 cm) cinnamon stick
2-inch (5 cm) stalk lemongrass
¼ teaspoon fenugreek seeds

1. Rinse and dry fish. Rub with lime juice, salt, and turmeric and set aside.

2. Heat oil in pan. Sauté onions, garlic, and green chilies until onions are translucent. Add fish, coconut milk, water, and all other ingredients. Bring to a boil, then reduce heat and simmer for 7 to 8 minutes until done.

MAKES 6 TO 8 SERVINGS

Fish Mustard Curry
Abba Kiri Malu

Mustard adds a tangy note to this popular fish dish.

1 pound (454 g) white fish steaks or
  fillets, cut into 1-inch chunks
2 tablespoons oil
1 onion, sliced
3 Serrano chilies or 1 green pepper,
  sliced into rings
1-inch (2.5 cm) cinnamon stick
2-inch (5 cm) stalk lemongrass
5 cloves
1 sprig curry leaves
½ cup water
½ cup (125 ml) coconut milk
¼ teaspoon turmeric powder
1 teaspoon salt
juice of one lime

SPICE PASTE:
1½ teaspoons black mustard seeds
¼ teaspoon ground black pepper
½ teaspoon fennel seeds
2 cloves garlic
2-inch (5-cm) piece ginger
½ tablespoon shredded coconut
1 tablespoon vinegar
½ teaspoon sugar

1. Wash and pat dry fish. Grind spice paste ingredients in a mortar and pestle or food processor. Rub into fish and set aside for 30 minutes.

2. Heat oil in pan. Sauté onions, chilies, cinnamon stick, lemongrass, cloves, and curry leaves until onion is translucent. Add fish and toss for 2 minutes. Add the water, bring to a boil, then reduce heat and simmer for 5 to 7 minutes.

3. Add coconut milk, turmeric powder, and salt and simmer for an additional 5 minutes. Squeeze with juice of lime before serving.

MAKES 4 TO 6 SERVINGS

Sour Fish Curry
Fish Ambul Thiyal

This amazing dish, a remnant from the days of no refrigeration, only gets better with age. *Goraka* (Garcinia gamboge) a sour, orange, kidney-shaped fruit that turns black when dried, is the secret ingredient that imparts its signature tart taste while also acting as an excellent preservative. You should be able to source this ingredient online or at any Sri Lankan store. It also comes as a ready-made paste with salt and garlic included. Great flavor along with ease of preparation makes this one of my all-time favorite dishes.

NOTE: This is a dry curry with little or no gravy.

1 pound (454 g) fresh tuna steaks, cut into 1-inch cubes
5 pieces *goraka*, or 2 tablespoons *goraka* paste
1 teaspoon ground black pepper
1 teaspoon cayenne pepper powder
1½ teaspoons salt
2 tablespoons oil

1 onion, finely diced
4 cloves garlic, minced
2-inch (5 cm) piece ginger, minced
2-inch (2.5 cm) cinnamon stick
1 sprig curry leaves
2 green chilies, sliced
½ cup (125 ml) water

1. Rinse and pat dry tuna.

2. Soak *goraka* pieces in ¼ cup hot water for 20 minutes before grinding into a thick but smooth paste in a food processor or blender (if using the ready-made paste skip this step). Add black pepper, cayenne pepper powder, and salt and mix well. Coat fish with this marinade and set aside for 30 minutes.

3. Heat oil in a pan. Sauté onions, garlic, ginger, cinnamon stick, curry leaves, and green chilies until onions are translucent.

4. Add the fish and water and bring to a boil. Reduce heat and simmer until all water has evaporated and fish is cooked through.

MAKES 4 TO 6 SERVINGS

Shark Curry
Mora Kalupol

Shark is a firm, meaty fish that soaks up the flavors of the ingredients, but swordfish works equally well for this dish. The *kalupol* method, which literally means 'blackened coconut,' uses roasted shredded coconut to make a thick, smoky base for the gravy.

1 pound (454 g) shark or swordfish steak, cut into 1-inch cubes
2 pieces *goraka*; or 1 tablespoon fresh tamarind, soaked in warm water, with fiber and seeds strained
3 tablespoons shredded coconut, fresh or dessicated
1 to 2 teaspoons cayenne pepper powder
2 teaspoons cumin powder
2 teaspoons coriander powder

½ teaspoon fennel powder
3 cloves garlic, minced
2-inch (5 cm) piece ginger, minced
2 tablespoons oil
1 onion, sliced
1 sprig curry leaves
2 to 3 green chilies, sliced
1-inch (2.5 cm) cinnamon stick
¼ cup (50 ml) water
salt to taste

1. Rinse and dry shark or swordfish steak.

2. Soak *goraka* in ¼ cup hot water for 20 minutes, and then grind to a paste in food processor or blender.

3. In a small pan, dry roast coconut until browned. Add cayenne pepper powder, cumin powder, coriander powder, and fennel powder and and mix well.

4. Add the dry-roasted ingredients, garlic and ginger to the *goraka* paste in the food processor and grind to make a thick paste. Coat fish well with paste and set aside to marinate for about 30 minutes.

5. Heat oil in pan. Sauté onions, curry leaves, green chilies, and cinnamon stick until onions are translucent. Add fish and stir-fry for 2 to 3 minutes. Add water and salt and bring to a boil. Then reduce heat and simmer for about 20 to 25 minutes.

MAKES 4 TO 6 SERVINGS

RICE & CURRY

VEGETABLES, LEGUMES, FRUITS & NUTS

As part of their daily diets, Sri Lankans consume large amounts of fresh fruits and vegetables, many of which are not even known or available in the west. Fleshy jackfruit, mineral-packed *gotu kola* leaves, and crunchy lotus root are among the many unique offerings found at colorful produce markets here that make it onto the dining table. For a rice & curry meal invariably features several vegetables to complement one or two meat or fish curries. Generally speaking, vegetable curries are made with raw curry powder for a much milder flavor.

Sri Lankan Lentils
Dal/Parippu

No Sri Lankan meal would be complete without these high-protein legumes, which soak up the flavors of coconut milk, lemongrass, and cinnamon. When eaten with rice, they comprise a perfect protein. You can vary the consistency of the lentils from thick as oatmeal to watery as soup, depending on how much water you add. Throw in some fresh spinach leaves at the end for added color, flavor, and vitamins.

½ pound (226 g) lentils
2 cups (500 ml) water
½ onion, diced
2 to 3 green chilies, sliced
2 cloves garlic, sliced
1-inch piece ginger, minced
1-inch (2.5 cm) piece pandan leaf (optional)
1-inch (2.5 cm) stalk lemongrass
1-inch (2.5 cm) cinnamon stick
1 cardamom pod
1 clove
½ teaspoon turmeric powder
½ cup (125 ml) coconut milk
salt to taste

FOR TEMPERING:
2 tablespoons oil
½ onion, sliced
1 sprig curry leaves
1 teaspoon black mustard seeds
2 whole dry red chilies

1. Wash and drain lentils removing any stones or chaff.

2. Boil the water in a medium-size pot. Add lentils, onion, green chilies, garlic, ginger, pandan leaf, lemongrass, cinnamon stick, cardamom pods, and clove. Simmer until lentils are soft, about 20 minutes, stirring occasionally.

3. Add turmeric, coconut milk, and salt. Cook for an additional 5 minutes.

4. **FOR TEMPERING:** In another pan, heat oil. Sauté onions and curry leaves until onions are translucent. Add mustard seeds and dry chilies. Fry until mustard seeds start to pop. Pour over lentils and mix well before serving.

MAKES 4 TO 6 SERVINGS

Carrot Curry
Karat Kirata

This mild white curry adds a burst of color to any rice and curry menu.

½ pound (227 g) carrots
2 tablespoons oil
1 onion, sliced
2 to 3 green chilies, sliced on the
  bias
1 sprig curry leaves
2-inch piece pandan leaf (optional)
1 tablespoon raw curry powder
1 dry red chili, chopped

1 teaspoon Maldive fish (or tiny dry
  shrimp from any Asian market)
¼ teaspoon fenugreek seeds
½ teaspoon turmeric powder
1 cup (250 ml) coconut milk
½ cup water
salt to taste
1 teaspoon mustard or ground black
  mustard seeds

1. Wash, peel, and slice carrots into thin half-moons.

2. Heat oil in pan. Sauté onions, green chilies, and curry leaves until onions are translucent. Add carrots and pandan leaf, curry powder, dry red chili, Maldive fish, fenugreek seeds, and turmeric powder and toss for a few minutes.

3. Add ½ cup of the coconut milk, the water and some salt and simmer for about 10 to 15 minutes until carrots are tender.

4. Add the remaining ½ cup of coconut milk and the mustard or mustard seeds, and simmer for an additional 5 minutes.

MAKES 4 TO 6 SERVINGS

Potato Curry
Ala Curry

This very mild curry is a favorite among children. It also adds just the right balance to a meal filled with spicier fare.

2 pounds (1 kg) potatoes
1 onion, sliced
2 to 3 green chilies, sliced
1 sprig curry leaves
¾ teaspoon fenugreek seeds

¾ teaspoon turmeric powder
1½ cups (375 ml) water
½ cup (125 ml) coconut milk
salt to taste

1. Wash, peel, and dice potatoes.

2. Place all ingredients except coconut milk and salt into a pan and bring to a boil. Reduce heat and simmer until potatoes are soft (about 15 to 20 minutes).

3. Add coconut milk and salt and simmer an additional 5 minutes.

MAKES 4 TO 6 SERVINGS

Beetroot Curry
Ratu Ala Curry

This hearty root vegetable makes for a robust and attractive curry. Plus, beets have a whole host of health benefits, including lowering blood pressure, fighting inflammation, and supporting heart, brain, and digestive functions.

1 pound (454 g) beetroots, washed, peeled, and cut into 1-inch sticks
2 tablespoons oil
1 onion, sliced
1 sprig curry leaves
2 to 3 green chilies, sliced

1 tablespoon raw curry powder
1 teaspoon cayenne pepper powder
2-inch (5 cm) cinnamon stick
3 teaspoons vinegar
1 cup (250 ml) coconut milk
salt to taste

1. Par cook beets in a pan of water with ½ teaspoon salt (water should completely cover beets) for 10 to15 minutes until almost tender. Drain and set aside.

2. Heat oil in pan. Fry onions, curry leaves, and green chilies until onions are translucent. Add curry powder, cayenne pepper powder, and cinnamon stick and sauté for an additional 2 minutes.

3. Add beets and vinegar. Mix well. Add coconut milk and simmer for an additional 5 minutes, adding salt to taste.

MAKES 4 TO 6 SERVINGS

Spinach Curry
Nivithi Curry

This curry, rich in iron and minerals, comes together very quickly, making it a perfect side dish.

1 pound (454 g) spinach
2 tablespoons oil
1 onion, sliced
2 cloves garlic, sliced
2 to 3 green chilies, sliced
1 sprig curry leaves

1 teaspoon coriander powder
¼ teaspoon turmeric powder
¼ cup (65 ml) coconut milk
¼ cup (65 ml) water
salt to taste

1. Wash and chop spinach.

2. Heat oil in pan. Add onions, garlic, green chilis, and curry leaves, and sauté until onions are translucent. Add coriander and turmeric and stir-fry an additional 2 minutes.

3. Add coconut milk and water and bring to a boil. Reduce heat and toss in spinach and cook until wilted.

MAKES 4 TO 6 SERVINGS

Sautéed Greens
Mallung

For this quick and simple preparation of greens, feel free to use kale, kohlrabi, mustard greens, turnip greens, beet greens, chard, or collards. I prefer a combination of collards and kale.

1 bunch (about 1 pound) greens, stems removed
1 tablespoon oil
1 onion, sliced
½ teaspoon black mustard seeds

2 to 3 tablespoons shredded coconut, fresh, frozen, or desiccated (unsweetened)
¼ teaspoon turmeric powder
Salt and pepper to taste
juice of one lime

1. Wash and dry greens. Finely chop or shred (you should have about 4 cups).

2. Heat oil in pan and sauté onions until translucent. Add mustard seeds and cook for 1 minute until they begin to pop.

3. Add greens, coconut, and turmeric powder and toss well adding a little water. Cook for 2 to 3 minutes. Season with salt and pepper. Squeeze lime juice over just before serving.

MAKES 4 TO 6 SERVINGS

RICE & CURRY

Cabbage Mallung

½ teaspoon black mustard seeds
½ teaspoon turmeric powder
½ cup coconut, freshly shredded, frozen, or desiccated
2 tablespoons oil
1 onion, sliced

2 green chilies, sliced
½ pound (227 g) cabbage, finely shredded
2 dry red chilies, broken into pieces
¼ cup water
Salt to taste

1. In a mortar and pestle, roughly grind black mustard seeds, turmeric, and coconut. Set aside.

2. Heat oil in pan. When hot, stir-fry onions and green chilies until onion is translucent.

3. Add cabbage, red chilies, and water and cook, covered for 10 minutes, until cabbage is tender. Add the ground ingredients and salt to taste, mix well, and cook for an additional 5 minutes. Remove from heat and serve immediately.

MAKES 4 TO 6 SERVINGS

French Green Bean Curry
Bonchi Curry

This very mild curry would not be out of place on a menu consisting of Western dishes.

1 pound (454 g) French green beans
2 tablespoons oil
1 onion, sliced
2 to 3 green chilies, sliced
1 sprig curry leaves

1 tablespoon raw curry powder
¼ teaspoon turmeric powder
½ cup (125 ml) coconut milk
½ cup (125 ml) water
salt to taste

1. Wash beans and slice on the bias into 2-inch pieces.

2. Heat oil in pan. Sauté onions, green chilies, and curry leaves until onions are translucent.

3. Add raw curry powder and sauté 1 minute. Add beans, turmeric, coconut milk, water, and salt.

4. Simmer for about 30 minutes until beans are tender and most of the liquid has evaporated.

MAKES 4 TO 6 SERVINGS

Cashew Nut Curry
Cadju Curry

A favorite in Sri Lanka where cashews are plentiful, this signature dish of Sri Lankan cuisine is often served to Buddhist monks at almsgivings or for other special occasions. Remember not to use roasted cashews!

½ pound (227 g) raw cashew nuts
1½ cups (375 ml) water
½ teaspoon turmeric powder
1 teaspoon ghee
1 onion, chopped
2 cloves garlic, minced
2-inch (5 cm) piece ginger, minced

2-inch (5 cm) stalk lemongrass
2 to 3 green chilies, sliced
1 sprig curry leaves
1 tablespoon raw curry powder
1 cup (250 ml) coconut milk
salt to taste

1. Soak cashews in water to cover overnight (changing water at least once). Drain.

2. Boil cashews in water with turmeric until tender, about 10 to 15 minutes. Drain.

3. Heat ghee in a pan. Fry onions, garlic, ginger, lemongrass, green chilies, and curry leaves until onions are translucent.

4. Add curry powder, coconut milk, salt, and cooked cashews. Cook on medium heat until liquid has almost evaporated.

MAKES 4 TO 6 SERVINGS

Moong Bean Curry
Moong Ata

A legume similar to lentils, moong beans are an alternative to *parippu* (dal). Popular in rural areas, this dish is an excellent source of protein, packed with vitamins and minerals.

8 ounces (227 g) dry moong beans
2 tablespoons oil
1 onion, diced
2 to 3 green chilies
1 sprig curry leaves
1 to 2 teaspoons cayenne pepper
  powder

½ teaspoon cumin powder
¼ teaspoon turmeric powder
1 cup (250 ml) coconut milk
½ cup (125 ml) water
salt to taste

1. Soak beans overnight with water to cover (changing water at least once). Drain.

2. Heat oil in pan. Sauté onions, green chilies, and curry leaves until onions are translucent.

3. Add powdered spices and stir-fry for a minute.

4. Add moong beans, coconut milk, water, and salt. Bring to a boil, then reduce heat and simmer until beans are tender, about 30 minutes.

MAKES 2 TO 4 SERVINGS

Aunty Manel's Special Eggplant Curry
Vambotu Curry

This dish is probably the tastiest preparation of eggplant, popularly known in Sri Lanka as brinjals, that you will ever eat. Though a little labor intensive and time-consuming, it's well worth the effort. Rubbing the eggplant with salt and turmeric and allowing it to drain for 30 minutes removes any bitterness and excess moisture.

1 pound (454 g) eggplant, washed
  and cut into 2-inch strips
2 teaspoons salt
½ teaspoon turmeric powder
oil for deep-frying
2 tablespoons oil
1 onion, sliced
2 to 3 green chilies, sliced
1 sprig curry leaves
2-inch (5 cm) cinnamon stick
3 cloves
1 tablespoon roasted curry powder
1 to 2 teaspoons cayenne pepper
  powder

¼ cup (65 ml) coconut milk (optional)
salt to taste

SPICE PASTE:
3 cloves garlic
2-inch (5 cm) piece ginger
1 teaspoon black mustard seeds;
  or 1 teaspoon spicy mustard
1 teaspoon sugar
1 teaspoon salt
1 tablespoon apple cider vinegar
½ cup (125 ml) water

1. Rub eggplant strips with salt and turmeric and allow to drain in colander for 30 minutes. Rinse and pat dry with paper towels.

2. Heat oil in a pot. Deep-fry eggplant until golden brown. Drain on paper towels laid on a wire rack. (Alternatively, for a healthier version, instead of deep-frying, you can spray the eggplant with oil to coat and bake in the oven at 350 degrees F for 45 minutes, flipping halfway.)

3. Blend spice paste ingredients in a food processor or blender to form a thin paste.

4. Heat oil in pan. Sauté onions, green chilies, and curry leaves until onions are translucent. Add cinnamon stick, cloves, curry powder, and cayenne pepper powder.

5. Add spice paste and bring to a boil. Reduce heat and add eggplant, coconut milk (if using), and salt to taste. Toss well and simmer for 3 to 5 minutes allowing the eggplant to soak up the flavor.

MAKES 4 TO 6 SERVINGS

Okra Curry
Bandakka Curry

This quick preparation of okra minimizes the sliminess of this vegetable when cooked, but make sure it is stir-fried well before adding the liquids.

1 pound (454 g) okra
2 tablespoons oil
1 onion, sliced
2 to 3 green chilies, sliced
1 sprig curry leaves
¼ teaspoon turmeric powder
½ teaspoon fenugreek seeds

1 tablespoon raw curry powder
½ cup (125 ml) coconut milk
¼ cup (65 ml) water
salt to taste

1. Wash okra, cut off tops, and slice diagonally into 1-inch (2.5 cm) pieces.

2. Heat oil in pan. Sauté onions, green chilies, and curry leaves until onions are translucent. Add turmeric, fenugreek seeds, and curry powder and stir well. Add okra and stir-fry for 2 to 3 minutes.

3. Add coconut milk, water, and salt and simmer until okra is tender (about 10 minutes).

MAKES 4 TO 6 SERVINGS

Spiced Potatoes
Ala Thel Dala

A crowd pleaser in Sri Lanka, this spicy, savory dish completes any menu. It is well worth the effort to find some Maldive fish, which in addition to its flavor, adds a nice textural counterpoint to the tender potatoes.

2 large potatoes, peeled and diced
2 tablespoons oil
1 onion, sliced
1 sprig curry leaves
2 dry red chilies, ground; or 1 to 2
  teaspoons dried cayenne pepper
  flakes

1 teaspoon Maldive fish (optional)
¼ teaspoon turmeric powder
salt to taste
juice of one lime

1. Bring water to boil in a medium pot. Add potato pieces and boil for 5 to 7 minutes. Drain and set aside.

2. Heat oil in pan. Sauté onions and curry leaves until onions are translucent.

3. Add potatoes, ground chilies or cayenne pepper flakes, Maldive fish, turmeric, and salt. Stir-fry for several minutes.

4. Squeeze lime juice over before serving.

MAKES 4 TO 6 SERVINGS

A Trip to a
Sri Lankan Market

Sri Lanka certainly boasts its fair share of modern supermarkets—namely such island-wide chains as Keel's and Cargill's Food City. Though nothing like the lavish über-stocked megastores in the U.S., they still offer some semblance of western-style grocery shopping in a neat and organized setting. But to really get a taste of how most of the local populace shops, you need go no further than any main street. On the bustling thoroughfares of Colombo, all manner of street vendors peddle their wares on sometimes nothing more than a sackcloth laid out on the pavement. Since they tend to congregate next to each other, you'll find dozens of impromptu street markets, chock full of produce, meat, fish, and housewares. Additionally, several long-established covered markets around town featuring semi-permanent stalls

RED BANANA

offer a farmers' market feel with fresh, seasonal produce to match. No imported Peruvian asparagus or oranges from South Africa here, but rather mountains of local mangoes or pyramids of pineapple stacked neatly next to more obscure fruits and vegetables. In Sri Lanka, 'local' and 'sustainable' are not simply trendy buzzwords, but rather the norm.

The best part about shopping at open-air markets is being able to see, smell, touch, and taste the food you are eventually going to ingest. Bargaining is welcomed, but hardly necessary considering the comparatively low prices. One should also take full advantage of the opportunity to try a whole host of products that you would never be able to find at home—foods like *gotu kola*, jackfruit, and *rambutan*. *Gotu kola*, a small green plant from the parsley family with thin stalks and rounded leaves, somewhat akin to cilantro, is typically used in *mallung* (page 151), a quick and easy side dish for rice and curry.

Speaking of curries, *polos* (young jackfruit) is a personal favorite. The oblong-shaped jackfruit, with an almost neon green hue and covered with hard 'scales,' is the largest tree-borne fruit in the world, sometimes reaching 80 pounds in weight, up to 36 inches in length, and 20 inches in diameter. Mature jackfruit, known as *kos* in Sri Lanka, has a sweet flavor and may be eaten raw. Young jackfruit, on the other hand, has a more bitter taste, but soaks up the flavor of whatever it is cooked in. With its fleshy texture it has been used as a substitute for meat (i.e. vegan pulled pork).

RIPE JACKFRUIT FLESH

GOTU KOLA, MANIOC, PUMPKIN, AVOCADO

As far as fruits go, I gorge myself on mainstays like mangoes, papayas, and pine-apple, but *rambutan* ranks as a childhood favorite. Certainly unique in appearance their bright, red color and bristly skin has earned them the nickname 'hairy balls in my family. Peeling off this outer layer reveals a sweet, tender white core remi-niscent of a lichi fruit that tastes divine. While much of this produce may not be 'certified organic' according to western standards, many small farmers who peddle their crops cannot afford expensive chemical fertilizers and pesticides. As a result fruits and vegetables in Sri Lanka taste how they're supposed to taste and not like flavorless facsimiles.

MANGOSTEEN

In addition to produce, meat, poultry, and fish are also sold at street markets. But unlike the sanitized supermarket version—packaged in shrink-wrap and Styrofoam—freshly gutted carcasses and parts are hung up without refrigeration or protection from the flies, heat, and dust. Squawking crows congregate on telephone wires, greedily waiting for a scrap, but nothing goes to waste as all parts of the animal (including the offal or innards) are for sale. *Barbath*, or tripe (cow's stomach), which looks like some kind of honeycombed sponge, is a real delicacy here. Even fish and seafood are not put on ice as they sell out quickly. The most they can hope for is a dousing of cold water to prevent them from drying out in the sun. But all the blood and guts offer an implicit guarantee that these animals have been killed or caught on the very same day that they go to market. They will probably be cooked and eaten on that same day as well. Despite enjoying the modern luxury of refrigeration at home, Sri Lankans prize fresh food and will make daily trips to the market because old habits die hard.

For the uninitiated, a trip to a Sri Lankan street market offers an eye opening, albeit sometimes scary, experience. Regardless, the sights, sounds, tastes, smells, and people-watching provide an excellent way to get at the heart of this culture, and this applies to anywhere in the world.

BITTER GOURD

Mushroom Curry
Hathu Curry

Despite the prevalence of mushrooms in Sri Lanka, they are not as popular as they are in other Asian cuisines. But cooked mushrooms have a meaty texture and soak up a lot of flavor, so this dish should not be missed.

2 pounds (1 kg) cremini or white button mushrooms
2 tablespoons oil
1 onion, chopped
3 cloves garlic, sliced
2 to 3 green chilies, sliced
1 sprig curry leaves
1 teaspoon black mustard seeds

1 tablespoon raw curry powder
1 teaspoon coriander powder
1 teaspoon cayenne pepper powder
¼ teaspoon turmeric powder
2 medium tomatoes, blanched and diced
½ cup (125 ml) coconut milk
salt to taste

1. Wash mushrooms well and cut into quarters.

2. Heat oil in pan. Sauté onions, garlic, green chilies, and curry leaves until onions are translucent. Add mustard seeds and fry for 1 to 2 minutes until they start to pop.

3. Add mushrooms and all other ingredients. Bring to a boil, then reduce heat and simmer for 10 to 15 minutes.

MAKES 4 TO 6 SERVINGS

Cabbage Curry
Gova Curry

Cabbage, a member of the Brassic family, is an underrated vegetable for its numerous health benefits and ease of preparation. This dish, which comes together quickly, provides an excellent part of a rice & curry meal.

1 head of cabbage
1 onion, sliced
2 to 3 green chilies, sliced
1 tablespoon raw curry powder
1 teaspoon cayenne pepper powder
¼ teaspoon turmeric powder
½ cup (125 ml) water
½ cup (125 ml) coconut milk
 salt to taste

FOR TEMPERING:
2 tablespoons oil
1 onion, sliced
1 sprig curry leaves
1 teaspoon raw curry powder
½ teaspoon black mustard seeds

1. Wash and shred cabbage, removing core.

2. Combine all ingredients (except ones for tempering) in a pan and cook until cabbage is tender, about 10 to 15 minutes.

3. **FOR TEMPERING:** Heat oil in a pan. Sauté onions and curry leaves until onions are translucent. Add curry powder and mustard seeds and fry another minute until seeds start to pop. Pour over cabbage and mix well.

MAKES 4 TO 6 SERVINGS

Sautéed Leeks
Leeks Temperadu

A member of the Allium family along with onions, garlic, chives, and shallots, leeks have an amazing flavor. But they must be cleaned thoroughly to remove the grit that sometimes gets lodged in between its layers. To do so, halve them lengthwise, then slice and toss in a bowl of cold water. The grit settles to the bottom, and you can scoop out the cleaned leeks.

2 cups sliced leeks (white and light green parts only)
2 tablespoons oil or ghee
1 onion, sliced
2 cloves garlic, minced
2-inch (5 cm) piece ginger, minced
2 to 3 green chilies, sliced

1 sprig curry leaves
½ teaspoon red pepper flakes
1 tomato, blanched and diced
1 tablespoon raw curry powder
¼ teaspoon turmeric powder
1 teaspoon salt

1. Wash and clean leeks.

2. Heat oil in pan. Fry onions, garlic, ginger, green chilies, curry leaves, and red pepper flakes until onions are translucent.

3. Add leeks, tomato, curry powder, turmeric, and salt. Stir-fry on low heat for 5 to 7 minutes until leeks soften.

MAKES 4 TO 6 SERVINGS

Garlic Curry
Sudulunu Curry

As garlic is slow cooked in this dish, its usually strong odor and flavor mellows out. Tamarind adds a tangy note while a pinch of saffron adds some complexity.

4 heads garlic
2 tablespoons oil
1 teaspoon fenugreek seeds
5 or 6 small shallots, sliced
2 to 3 green chilies,
  slit from stem to tip
1 sprig curry leaves

1 teaspoon cayenne pepper powder
1 tablespoon fresh tamarind, soaked
  in ¼ cup warm water (straining
  seeds and fiber)
pinch of saffron
1 cup (250 ml) coconut milk
salt to taste

1. Separate garlic cloves and remove skin but keep cloves whole.

2. Heat oil in pan. Fry fenugreek seeds in hot oil for 2 minutes. Remove.

3. Fry garlic cloves, shallots, green chilies, and curry leaves for a few minutes.

4. Add cayenne pepper powder, tamarind water, saffron, and coconut milk to pan and bring to boil. Add fried fenugreek seeds, reduce heat and simmer until gravy thickens. Add salt to taste.

MAKES 4 TO 6 SERVINGS

Chickpea Curry
Kadalai Curry

This dish, of South Indian origin, comes from the north of the island, home to a predominantly Tamil population. It utilizes garam masala, a popular Indian spice mixture that is readily available at most US supermarkets today.

1 large potato, peeled and diced
2 (15 oz.) cans chickpeas, rinsed and
  drained
½ cup (125 ml) water
1-inch (2.5 cm) piece ginger
2 cloves garlic
¼ teaspoon turmeric powder
2 tablespoons oil

1 onion, sliced
1 sprig curry leaves
1 teaspoon Jaffna curry powder
  (page 51)
1 tomato, blanched and diced
salt to taste
1 teaspoon garam masala
juice of one lemon

1. Boil potato in salted water for 5 minutes. Drain and set aside.

2. Grind ¼ cup of the chickpeas, the water, ginger, garlic, and turmeric in food processor or blender. Set aside.

3. Heat oil in pan. Sauté onions and curry leaves until onions are translucent. Add curry powder and mix for a minute. Add remaining chickpeas and tomatoes, potatoes, and pureed chickpeas. Stir well and simmer until mixture is thick and creamy.

4. Add salt to taste and sprinkle with garam masala and squeeze with lemon juice before serving.

MAKES 4 TO 6 SERVINGS

Soya Curry

Just to demonstrate that anything can be curried, this recipe incorporates dried soya chunks (sometimes known as textured vegetable protein or TVP) that have become popular as a meat alternative.

12 ounces (340 g) dried soya chunks
2 teaspoons raw curry powder
1 to 2 teaspoons cayenne pepper
  powder
2 teaspoons chopped fresh ginger
3 cloves garlic
2 tablespoons oil
1 onion, sliced
2 to 3 green chilies, sliced

1-inch (2.5 cm) piece pandan leaf
  (optional)
1 sprig curry leaves
1 teaspoon fresh tamarind, soaked
  in ¼ cup warm water, then seeds
  and fiber strained
1 cup (250 ml) coconut milk
salt to taste

1. Soak soya in a bowl of boiling water for 10 minutes. Drain and squeeze out excess water. Toss with curry powder and cayenne pepper powder.

2. Grind ginger and garlic together in a mortar and pestle.

3. Heat oil in pan. Sauté garlic and ginger mixture, onions, green chilies, pandan leaf, and curry leaves until onions are translucent.

4. Add seasoned soya chunks and stir-fry for 2 to 3 minutes.

5. Add tamarind water, coconut milk, and to salt to taste. Cook an additional 5 minutes until gravy reduces and thickens.

MAKES 4 TO 6 SERVINGS

Pineapple Curry
Anasi Curry

This unique curry that utilizes unripe (green) pineapple is bursting with flavors—sweet, spicy, and savory.

1 unripe pineapple
1 onion, sliced
2 green chilies, sliced
1-inch (2.5 cm) cinnamon stick
1 teaspoon coriander powder
1 teaspoon cumin powder

2 teaspoons cayenne pepper powder
1½ teaspoons ground black mustard
  seeds
½ cup (125 ml) coconut milk
1 teaspoon salt

1. Peel and cut pineapple into 1-inch pieces.

2. Mix all ingredients together in a small pot. Bring to a boil and simmer until pineapple is tender, about 20 minutes.

MAKES 4 TO 6 SERVINGS

Mango Curry
Amba Curry

Another unripe fruit curry proves that Sri Lankans will curry anything. Green mangoes, tart to the taste, along with coconut milk and spices, add up to a unique dish loaded with flavor.

2 firm green (unripe) mangoes
2 tablespoons oil
1 onion, sliced
3 cloves garlic, minced
2-inch (5 cm) piece ginger, minced
5 dried red chilies, chopped
2-inch (5 cm) piece pandan leaf
  (optional)
1-inch (2.5 cm) cinnamon stick
2-inch (5 cm) stalk lemongrass
1 sprig curry leaves

1 teaspoon black mustard seeds
1 tablespoon vinegar
1 tablespoon sugar
¼ teaspoon turmeric powder
3 cloves
1 cup (250 ml) water
2 tablespoons raw curry powder
1 to 2 teaspoons cayenne pepper
  powder
½ cup (125 ml) coconut milk
salt to taste

1. Wash and peel mangoes and cut into chunks. Prick with fork and cover in salted water for 30 minutes. Drain.

2. Heat oil in pan. Sauté onions, garlic, ginger, chilies, pandan leaf, cinnamon stick, lemongrass, and curry leaves until onions are translucent. Add mustard seeds and sauté for a minute more until they start to pop.

3. Add mango, vinegar, sugar, turmeric, cloves, and water and bring to a boil. Reduce heat and simmer for 10 to 15 minutes.

4. In another pan, roast curry powder and cayenne pepper powder until fragrant. Mix in coconut milk and add to mango.

5. Stir gently and add salt to taste. Cook for 5 more minutes until all flavors are incorporated.

MAKES 4 TO 6 SERVINGS

Yellow Pumpkin Curry
Vattakka Curry

Though the pumpkins look slightly different in Sri Lanka, I think any type of pumpkin, or even butternut squash, would work for this dish.

1 pound (454 g) pumpkin, peeled
   and cubed in 1-inch chunks
2 tablespoons oil
1 onion, sliced
2 to 3 green chilies, sliced
1 sprig curry leaves
¾ cup (185 ml) coconut milk
1 teaspoon salt

SPICE PASTE:
1 tablespoon shredded coconut,
   fresh, frozen, or desiccated
   (unsweetened)
¼ teaspoon turmeric powder
½ teaspoon black mustard seeds
2 cloves garlic, minced
1 teaspoon minced ginger

1. Par cook pumpkin chunks in a pot of water for 10 to 15 minutes until almost tender. Remove and drain.

2. Grind spice paste ingredients together with mortar and pestle.

3. Heat oil in pan. Sauté onions, green chilies, and curry leaves until onions are translucent.

4. Add pumpkin, coconut milk, salt, and spice paste mixture and mix well. Simmer for 10 minutes until pumpkin is tender and gravy thickens.

MAKES 4 TO 6 SERVINGS

Cauliflower Curry
Gova Mal Curry

Since cauliflower, a member of the Brassica family, is not native to Sri Lanka, it is considered somewhat exotic, and is therefore only served on special occasions. But why not celebrate how tasty this humble vegetable can be?

1 head cauliflower
½ pound (226 g) green peas
2 tablespoons oil
1 onion, sliced
2 to 3 green chilies, sliced
1 sprig curry leaves
1 teaspoon black mustard seeds
2 medium tomatoes, blanched,
  skinned, and diced

2 tablespoons raw curry powder
1 teaspoon cayenne pepper powder
½ teaspoon turmeric powder
½ cup (125 ml) water
½ cup (125 ml) coconut milk
salt to taste

1. Wash and cut cauliflower into florets.

2. Boil peas in water to cover until tender. Drain and set aside.

3. Heat oil in pan. Sauté onions, green chilies, and curry leaves until onion is translucent. Add mustard seeds and fry until they pop (about 1 minute).

4. Add tomatoes, curry powder, cayenne powder, and turmeric powder and mix well. Add cauliflower florets and mix well.

5. Add water, coconut milk, and salt and bring to a boil. Reduce heat and simmer until cauliflower is tender, about 10 to 15 minutes.

6. Mix in cooked green peas before serving.

MAKES 4 TO 6 SERVINGS

Lotus Root Badun

The beautiful lotus flower rises from the beds of ponds and lakes and snakes up to the surface. Its roots are a unique treat enjoyed all over Asia. But imagine my surprise when I came across fresh lotus roots in the produce department of H-Mart, a Korean supermarket chain in the U.S. If you can't find fresh ones, you can certainly buy them canned at any Asian store.

1 pound fresh or canned lotus root
2 to 3 teaspoons Maldive fish flakes (optional)
⅛ teaspoon turmeric powder
1 medium red onion, sliced
2 to 3 green chilies, sliced
1 to 2 teaspoons cayenne pepper powder

1 tablespoon raw curry powder
1 cup (250 ml) coconut milk
2 tablespoons oil
2 cloves garlic, minced
1 sprig curry leaves
½ teaspoon black mustard seeds
Salt to taste

1. Boil the fresh lotus root in salted water until tender, about 10 to 15 minutes. Drain, remove skin and cut into thin slices. (If using canned, just drain and slice.)

2. Place lotus root slices in a medium saucepan along with Maldive fish, turmeric, half the onion slices, green chilies, half the cayenne pepper powder, curry powder, and coconut milk. Bring to a boil and then simmer for about 15 minutes, stirring occasionally.

3. Heat oil in small pan. Add the remaining onion slices, garlic, and curry leaves and sauté until onions are translucent. Add the mustard seeds and fry for 1 minute more until they begin to pop.

4. Add tempered ingredients to lotus root along with the remaining cayenne pepper powder and salt to taste. Mix well and cook for another 2 minutes.

MAKES 4 TO 6 SERVINGS

Young Jackfruit Curry
Polos Ambula

Though jackfruit is cultivated all over the island, this signature dish of Sri Lankan cuisine uses canned young jackfruit in brine, available at Trader Joe's and other fine western supermarkets. Obviously, use fresh jackfruit if you can get it, but this dish is cooked long enough and with sufficient spices to impress even the most discernable palate. If you've never had young jackfruit, its texture might even fool you into thinking you were eating meat.

2 cans (14-ounce each) brined jackfruit
1 tablespoon fresh tamarind, soaked in ¼ cup warm water with fiber and seeds strained
2 tablespoons oil
1 medium onion, sliced
3 cloves garlic, sliced
2-inch piece ginger, shredded
1 sprig curry leaves

2-inch piece pandan leaf (optional)
2-inch cinnamon stick
½ teaspoon turmeric powder
½ teaspoon fenugreek seeds
1 to 2 teaspoons cayenne pepper powder
1 teaspoon ground black pepper
2 tablespoons roasted curry powder
1 teaspoon salt

1. Rinse and drain jackfruit and prepare tamarind.

2. Heat oil in pan. When smoking add onions, garlic, ginger, curry leaves, pandan leaf, and cinnamon stick. Stir-fry until onions are translucent.

3. Add dry spices and salt and stir-fry an additional 2 minutes, being careful not to burn the spices.

4. Deglaze pan with some water and add jackfruit chunks and tamarind. Stir to combine. Reduce heat to low and add enough water to cover jackfruit.

5. Cook uncovered for approximately 30 to 45 minutes until liquid has reduced and jackfruit is tender. Add more water as necessary.

MAKES 4 TO 6 SERVINGS

Breadfruit Curry
Del Maluwa Curry

Breadfruit comes from the same family as jackfruit, so it makes sense that they would share a similar appearance (though jackfruit grows much bigger). Breadfruit is starchier, but like its cousin, soaks up the flavor of whatever you cook it in. You might be able to source fresh breadfruit from an Asian or Caribbean supermarket, otherwise canned is permissible. If you do manage to get a couple grapefruit-size fruit, cut off the tops and bottoms and remove all the green skin. Then quarter the fruit and remove the thick core before cutting it into uniform, bite-size chunks.

2 grapefruit-size breadfruit, peeled,
  cored, and cut into chunks or
  1 (14-ounce) can breadfruit
1 medium onion, diced
1 sprig curry leaves
2-inch piece pandan leaf (optional)
2 cloves garlic, minced
½ teaspoon fenugreek seeds
½ teaspoon turmeric powder
1 teaspoon cayenne pepper powder
1 teaspoon ground black pepper
1 teaspoon salt
1½ cups water
1 can (14-ounce) coconut milk

FOR TEMPERING:
2 tablespoons oil
1 medium onion, sliced
2-inch piece pandan leaf (optional)
1 sprig curry leaves
2 whole dry red chilies
1 teaspoon black mustard seeds

1. Place all ingredients (except coconut milk and those for tempering) in a pan and bring to a boil. Lower heat and let cook for 20 to 25 minutes until breadfruit is tender, stirring occasionally.

2. Add coconut milk, cover pot, and cook for 10 minutes until gravy thickens.

3. For tempering, heat oil in a small skillet. Add onion, pandan and curry leaves, and chilies and stir-fry until onions are translucent. Add mustard seeds and cook for another minute until they start to pop. Transfer tempered ingredients to pot with the breadfruit and mix well before serving.

MAKES 4 TO 6 SERVINGS

Boiled Manioc

Manioc, otherwise known as yucca or cassava, is a waxy tuberous root native to South America, but cultivated all throughout the tropical and subtropical regions of the world, from Africa to Asia. The Portuguese first introduced it to Sri Lanka, where it has become a popular starch, containing trace amounts of calcium and vitamin C. It is usually simply boiled and eaten for breakfast along with some coconut *sambol*.

NOTE: Since the thick skin on manioc contains cyanide it must be completely removed before preparation. Use a sharp chef knife since the flesh is difficult to cut through. Start by removing both ends and cutting it in half. Then stand each half on a cutting board, slicing downwards until all the skin is removed. Proceed by slicing each half down the center and carefully remove the thin fibrous strand before cutting it into uniform chunks.

1 to 2 pounds manioc
water
salt to taste

1. Clean and cut manioc, placing chunks in a bowl of water to soak for about 30 minutes. Rinse and strain.

2. Bring a pot of water to boil and add salt. Submerge the manioc chunks and cook until tender, about 15 to 30 minutes, depending on the size of the chunks.

3. Strain manioc and serve hot, adding a pad of butter for flavor and your favorite Sri Lankan condiment—Coconut Sambol (*Pol Sambol*; page 201), Onion Chili Sambol (*Lunu Miris*; page 202), or Sugar Sambol (*Seeni Sambol*; page 197).

MAKES 1 TO 2 SERVINGS

CHUTNEYS, PICKLES, SAMBOLS & SALADS

The condiments on a Sri Lankan table complement a meal by adding a touch of sweetness or acidity or a kiss of heat to round out the total palette of flavors. Typically, a rice and curry meal will cover the entire spectrum of tastes—sweet, sour, salty, bitter, and spicy. The chutneys, pickles, *sambols*, and salads that Sri Lankans savor are important details not to omit when serving this food. *Sambols* and salads typically utilize fresh, raw ingredients while the ingredients in most chutneys and pickles are boiled down and taste best aged.

Mango Chutney
Amba Chutney

Probably everyone's first introduction to chutney is mango, a sweet/sour counterpoint to an overall spicy meal. Choose mangoes that are green and firm when preparing this recipe.

4 unripe mangoes
 (about 2 pounds / 1 kg)
1 tablespoon chopped ginger
1 tablespoon chopped garlic
1 to 2 teaspoons cayenne pepper
 powder

1 tablespoon black mustard seeds
½ to ¾ cup (125-185 ml) distilled
 white vinegar
2 teaspoons salt
1 pound (454 g) sugar

1. Wash and peel mangoes and cut into small chunks.

2. Blend ginger, garlic, cayenne pepper powder, and mustard seeds in food processor or blender.

3. In a small pot, boil vinegar, salt, and sugar until sugar dissolves. Stir in mangoes and blended mixture. Boil until mangoes start to break down, about 45 to 60 minutes.

4. Remove from heat and pour directly into sterilized glass jars to cool. May be stored in the fridge for up to 3 months.

Pineapple Chutney
Anasi Chutney

A rarity in Sri Lanka despite its great flavor, pineapple chutney is only served on special occasions.

1 fresh pineapple
1 tablespoon chopped garlic
1 tablespoon chopped ginger
1 to 2 teaspoons cayenne pepper
  powder

1 tablespoon black mustard seeds
½ to ¾ cup (125-185 ml) vinegar
10 ounces (283 g) sugar
2 teaspoons salt
2-inch (5 cm) cinnamon stick

1. Cut off rind from pineapple, remove core, and dice fruit.

2. Blend garlic, ginger, cayenne pepper powder, and mustard seeds with a little of the vinegar in food processor or blender.

3. Boil remaining vinegar, sugar, salt, and cinnamon stick in a medium pot until sugar dissolves. Remove cinnamon stick after 5 minutes.

4. Add pineapple and blended mixture and simmer on medium heat for 45 to 60 minutes until it thickens.

5. Remove from heat and pour directly into sterilized glass jars to cool. May be stored in the fridge for up to 3 months.

Tamarind Chutney
Siyambala Chutney

This dark, rich chutney is pungent and sweet.

1 pound (454 g) tamarind pods
1 tablespoon chopped ginger
1 tablespoon chopped garlic
1 to 2 teaspoons cayenne pepper
  powder
1 tablespoon black mustard seeds

½ to ¾ cup (125-185 ml) distilled
  white vinegar
1 pound (454 g) sugar
2 teaspoons salt
½ pound (227 g) sultanas or raisins

1. Soak tamarind pods in a little warm water. Strain, removing seeds and fiber.

2. Grind ginger, garlic, cayenne pepper powder, and mustard seeds with a little of
the vinegar in a food processor or blender.

3. Boil remaining vinegar, sugar, and salt until sugar is dissolved. Add tamarind
and blended mixture and simmer for about 45 minutes, until mixture thickens.

4. Stir in raisins before removing from heat. Pour directly into sterilized glass jars
to cool. May be stored in the fridge for up to 3 months.

Date & Raisin Chutney
Rataindhi Chutney

This is one of my Aunt Padma's specialties. The sweetness of the dates and raisins mingled with the heat of cayenne and ginger and the acid of the vinegar creates a very complex flavor.

1 pound (454 g) dates
1 tablespoon chopped ginger
1 tablespoon chopped garlic
1 to 2 teaspoons cayenne pepper
  powder

1 to 2 teaspoons salt
1 cup (250 ml) vinegar
4 ounces (113 g) sugar
2-inch (5-cm) cinnamon stick
4 ounces (113 g) sultanas or raisins

1. Pit dates and cut into small pieces.

2. Blend ginger, garlic, cayenne pepper powder, salt, and a little of the vinegar in a food processor or blender.

3. In a small pot boil the rest of the vinegar and the sugar and cinnamon stick until sugar dissolves. Remove cinnamon stick after 5 minutes.

4. Add dates and blended mixture and mix well. Simmer until it thickens slightly. (**NOTE:** Mixture should be still a little watery, as it will thicken upon cooling.)

5. Add raisins before removing from heat. Pour directly into sterilized glass jars to cool. May be stored in the fridge for up to 3 months.

Coconut Chutney
Pol Chutney

Made with fresh coconut, this savory chutney goes especially well with Savory Donuts (*Ulundu Vadai*, page 64). If fresh coconut is not readily available, the next best thing is the shredded, frozen coconut "meat" that you get at Asian stores. Both simple to make and amazingly good, this condiment may be stored in the fridge for several days.

1 cup (250 ml) shredded
  fresh coconut
3 green chilies, chopped
1 teaspoon chopped ginger
1 tablespoon roasted chickpeas or
  peanuts
salt to taste

FOR TEMPERING:
1 tablespoon vegetable oil
4 curry leaves
1 whole dried red chili
1 teaspoon black mustard seeds
1 teaspoon urad dal
¼ teaspoon asafetida powder

1. Grind all ingredients (except those for tempering) in a blender or food processor. Add enough hot water to make a paste. Transfer paste to a bowl.

2. **FOR TEMPERING:** Heat oil in a pan and add curry leaves, chili, mustard seeds, urad dhal, and asafetida. Fry until mustard seeds start popping and turn gray, about 1 minute.

3. Add tempered ingredients to bowl of coconut paste and stir well. Chutney may be stored in the fridge for up to 3 days.

Mixed Pickle
Achcharu

The most commonly served pickle in Sri Lanka, supposedly of Malaysian origin, this condiment completes any rice & curry menu.

20 small shallots or
  cocktail onions, peeled
10 green chilies
¼ pound (113 g) green papaya
  (optional)
10 green beans
2 small carrots
¼ pound (113 g) cauliflower
1 cup (250 ml) distilled white vinegar
½ teaspoon salt

SPICE PASTE:
1 tablespoon chopped ginger
1 tablespoon chopped garlic
2 tablespoons sugar
1 tablespoon black mustard seeds
¼ teaspoon turmeric powder
¼ cup (65 ml) vinegar
1 tablespoon salt

1. Place shallots in salted water. Split green chilies from stem to tip. Peel papaya and cut into small strips. Cut beans and carrots into 1- to 2-inch (2.5-5cm) strips. Separate cauliflower into small florets.

2. Bring vinegar with salt to a boil. Cook each type of vegetable separately in the vinegar for 1 minute. Drain and set aside in a bowl together.

3. Grind spice paste ingredients in a blender or food processor. Pour over vegetables and mix well.

4. Store in a sterilized glass jar in the fridge for 2 to 3 days before using. Will keep for up to 3 months refrigerated.

Lime Pickle
Lunu Dehi

Though an acquired taste, lime pickle is probably the most popular condiment in Sri Lanka. Almost everyone likes a sliver of this pungent pickle to complement their plate of rice & curry.

10 limes
2 tablespoons coarse salt
1 cup (237 ml) lime juice

1. Wash and dry limes. Cut them into quarters without slicing all the way through, prick with fork in several places, and rub with salt. Leave the limes in a sterilized glass jar (with non-reactive lid) on the counter for 3 days.

2. Remove marinated limes from jar and spread out in a large shallow glass dish. Place in direct sunlight for 3 days until dry (cover with a loose cloth at night).

3. Place limes in a sterilized glass jar with non-reactive lid and pour lime juice over them. Seal and shake up jar and store in the refrigerator for 6 months before using. (Though limes will turn brown in color, they can be kept indefinitely.)

Sugar Sambol
Seeni Sambola

This savory/sweet relish, a perfect complement to milk rice, is a must on the breakfast table for Sri Lankan New Year. It also goes well with just about anything else.

2 tablespoons oil
1 pound (454 g) red onions, sliced
2 cloves garlic, minced
2-inch (5 cm) piece ginger, minced
1 sprig curry leaves
4 cardamom pods
3 cloves
2-inch (5 cm) cinnamon stick
2 teaspoons salt

2 teaspoons cayenne pepper powder
5 ounces (150 g) Maldive fish
5 tablespoons (75 g) fresh tamarind
    dissolved in ¼ cup (50 g) coconut
    milk and then fiber and seeds
    strained out and discarded
2 teaspoons sugar
juice of one lime

1. Heat oil in pan. Slowly fry onions, garlic, ginger, and curry leaves over low heat until onions are caramelized.

2. Add all other ingredients (except sugar and lime juice) and continue cooking on low heat for 30 to 45 minutes.

3. Add sugar and juice of lime and mix well just before taking off heat. Cool and store in a sterilized glass jar in the fridge for up to 3 days.

MAKES A 1 POUND (454 G) JAR

Chili Sambol
Katta Sambol

This seriously spicy condiment goes well with practically any Sri Lankan meal. The inclusion of Maldive fish gives it a unique flavor and chewy texture.

10 whole dried red chilies, stems removed

1 red onion, chopped

1 tablespoon Maldive fish

Juice of one lime

Salt to taste

1. Soak chilies in hot water for 15 minutes. Remove and drain. Grind chilies in a mortar and pestle. Add onions and Maldive fish and grind to a coarse paste.

2. Remove to a bowl and mix in lime juice and salt to taste. Store in a glass jar in the fridge for up to 3 days.

Coconut Sambol
Pol Sambol

Though sometimes known as the poor man's accompaniment to rice, coconut sambol is popular in every household. It goes great with hoppers (page 99) and other breads as well. Maldive fish, which may be sourced online or at a Sri Lankan grocer, adds a salty umami flavor and chewy texture. But if you can't get it, just leave it out, no problem.

1 onion, chopped
½ teaspoon black peppercorns
1 tablespoon Maldive fish flakes (or dried shrimp)
2 to 3 teaspoons cayenne pepper powder
1 to 2 green chilies, chopped

3 to 4 curry leaves, chopped (optional)
6 ounces (175 g) shredded coconut, fresh, frozen, or desiccated (unsweetened)
salt to taste
juice of one lime

1. Grind onions, peppercorns, and Maldive fish together in a mortar and pestle.

2. Mix remaining ingredients together in a bowl and add onion mixture. Adjust flavors to suite your own taste (adding more lime, salt, or chili as necessary). Store for up to 3 days in the fridge.

Onion Chili Sambol
Lunu Miris

This fiery mix of onions, chilies, and salty, chewy bits of Maldive fish is the perfect complement to hoppers (page 99) or Coconut Milk Rice (page 91).

1 onion, chopped
4 tablespoons dry red chilies
1 tablespoon Maldive fish flakes (or dried shrimp)

juice of one lime
salt to taste

Grind all ingredients together in a food processor or mortar and pestle to make a thick red paste. This sambol is best used on the day you make it, but it may be stored in the fridge for up to 3 days.

Mint Sambol
Minchi Sambol

This refreshing sambol is the perfect complement to lamb biriyani (page 94).

2 ounces (56 g) mint leaves
3 or 4 garlic cloves
2 or 3 peppercorns
2 or 3 green chilies

juice of 1 lime
pinch of sugar
salt to taste

1. Wash and pat dry mint leaves.

2. Grind all ingredients together in a food processor or blender to make a thick green paste. Store in a glass jar in the fridge for up to 3 days.

Carrot Sambol
Karat Sambol

This colorful dish, somewhere between a salad and a sambol since it is uncooked, is simultaneously cooling and spicy.

3 medium carrots
1 onion, finely chopped
1 tomato, chopped
2 to 3 green chilies, sliced
½ teaspoon salt

½ teaspoon pepper
3 tablespoons shredded
  unsweetened coconut, fresh,
  frozen, or desiccated
juice of one lime

1. Wash, peel, and grate carrots.

2. Place all ingredients in a bowl and mix well, adjusting salt and lime juice as desired. This sambol should be used within 2 to 3 days.

Radish and Tomato Sambol
Raabu Thakkali Sambol

Another cooling, spicy concoction.

1 pound (454 g) radishes, halved and
  thinly sliced
1 onion, sliced
2 to 3 green chilies, sliced
½ teaspoon sugar

½ teaspoon ground black pepper
1 teaspoon salt
1 tablespoon vinegar
3 tomatoes, quartered, seeded, and
  sliced

1. Soak radish slices in cold salted water for 10 minutes. Drain radishes and squeeze out excess water.

2. Mix all ingredients in a bowl, adding tomatoes last. Serve immediately.

Bitter Gourd Sambol
Karavila Sambol

Popular in Indian cooking, the bitter gourd resembles a small, prickly pickle. True to its name it has an astringent flavor, but soaking it in salt water neutralizes some of the bitterness.

1 pound (454 g) bitter gourd
oil for frying
1 onion, sliced
2 to 3 green chilies, sliced
1 dry red chili, sliced

1 tablespoon shredded unsweetened
  coconut, fresh, frozen, or desiccated
1 teaspoon salt
juice of one lime

1. Wash bitter gourd and slice into rounds. Soak in salted water for 20 to 30 minutes to remove some bitterness. Drain and pat dry.

2. Heat oil in pan. Deep fry bitter gourd until golden brown and crispy. Drain.

3. Place bitter gourd in a bowl and mix well with all the other ingredients. Serve immediately.

Tomato Cucumber Salad

This colorful and refreshing salad is a must for all rice and curry meals for its cooling effect, which complements spicy dishes.

2 medium tomatoes, quartered, seeded, and sliced
1 cucumber, halved, seeded, and sliced
½ red onion, sliced
2 to 3 green chilies, sliced on the bias

1 teaspoon Maldive fish flakes (optional)
1 hard-boiled egg, sliced (optional)
juice of one lime
salt to taste

Combine all ingredients in a bowl and mix well, being careful not to bruise the tomatoes. May be served immediately or kept in the fridge.

DESSERTS

The foreign influence on Sri Lankan cuisine seems to be the most prevalent when it comes to desserts. *Bolo de amor* (Love Cake) and Caramel Pudding, better known as crème caramel or flan, came from the Portuguese. *Broeder*, a Christmas fruitcake, and *kokis*, a kind of cookie, were contributions of the Dutch. The Christmas pudding that has become a holiday tradition on the island was a legacy of the British, and coconut flan came from the Malays. Bombay sweets from India, made with ghee, sugar, and milk powder, are also very popular on the island. You can add these to the wide range of local sweets that are enjoyed as well, most utilizing some form of coconut and *jaggery* (palm sugar). So, sweet-toothed Sri Lankans aren't picky about where they get their sugar fix. Sometimes a simple bowl of buffalo-milk curd and treacle (coconut syrup) offers the perfect ending to a spicy meal.

Ammi's Love Cake
Bolo de Amor

This very moist, rich, and fragrant cake is one of my mother's specialties, always made with lots of love. While somewhat labor intensive it does produce a cake like no other, which Sri Lankans usually enjoy with a cup of tea. And, no, the ten egg yolks that the recipe calls for is not a misprint.

1 pound (454 g) unsalted cashew nuts
½ pound (226 g) semolina
¼ pound (113 g) unsalted butter, cubed
10 egg yolks
1 pound (454 g) sugar

½ cup (125 ml) honey
½ teaspoon rose essence
¼ teaspoon grated nutmeg
¼ teaspoon grated lemon rind
¼ teaspoon ground cinnamon
¼ teaspoon ground allspice
1 tablespoon all-purpose flour

1. Roast cashews on medium heat. Cool and finely chop. Set aside.

2. Prepare a 9x12 pan with 4 layers of newspaper and 2 layers of parchment paper to prevent burning the sides and bottom of the cake. Butter parchment paper evenly or use a non-stick spray.

3. Preheat oven to 350 degrees F (175 degrees C).

4. In a medium saucepan, roast semolina. When warm, add butter and stir until melted and then cool.

5. Beat egg yolks in a large bowl for 1 minute. Add sugar and beat until creamy. Stir in honey, rose essence, nutmeg, lemon rind, cinnamon, and allspice. Add chopped cashews. Fold in semolina mixture and flour.

6. Pour into prepared pan and bake in oven until slightly golden and cooked in center, about 15 minutes.

7. Lower oven to 325 degrees F (160 degrees C) and bake for an additional 30 minutes or until a toothpick inserted into center comes out clean.

Caramel Pudding

This universally loved dessert, known by many names, such as flan or crème caramel, and found in many cultures is so easy to make—and even easier to eat. The Portuguese introduced it to Sri Lanka along with such other indispensable foods as the chili pepper, tomato, and potato.

2 to 3 tablespoons sugar
  (for caramel)
1 small can (14 oz/396 g) sweetened
  condensed milk

1½ cans water
4 eggs, beaten
few drops vanilla extract

1. Mix sugar with 1 tablespoon water in a 2-quart stainless steel mold and heat until golden. Swirl the melted sugar to coat base and sides.

2. In another bowl mix condensed milk, water, eggs, and vanilla.

3. Pour into prepared mold, cover with tin foil, and steam in a double boiler for 30 to 45 minutes until set. The water should not boil under it but simmer gently. (Alternatively, place the steel mold in another baking pan partially filled with water and bake in the oven at 350 F.)

4. Remove from heat and allow to cool. Once room temperature, cover and refrigerate for 5 to 6 hours before serving. You can either serve this from the mold or turn the pudding out onto a serving plate.

MAKES 6 TO 8 SERVINGS

Jaggery

Not all sugar is bad for you. Unrefined whole cane or palm sugar, commonly used throughout Asia, Africa, Latin America, and the Caribbean, provides an alternative to the highly processed white sugar available in the west. In Sri Lanka, this natural sweetener assumes the form of jaggery, a product derived from the *kithul* or fishtail palm tree *(Caryota urens)*, native to India, Sri Lanka, and Myanmar. Jaggery starts off as the milky sap extracted from its flowers, which quickly ferments into 'toddy' or 'palm wine.' After being boiled down with a little salt (as a preservative), it transforms into a dense, dark brown syrup that is poured into the split halves of coconut shells and cooled, giving it its characteristic bowl shape. Good jaggery has a dark brown color and a pliable consistency as opposed to lighter, harder product, which has probably been adulterated with sugar. If the toddy, or fermented sap, is not boiled down into jaggery, it is usually distilled in wooden vats to make Sri Lanka's liquor of choice, *Arrack* (from the Arabic for "strong liquor").

Full of minerals, such as calcium and phosphates, jaggery is much healthier than ordinary sugar because of its gradual release into the blood stream that does not cause a spike in blood sugar. In Ayurveda, it is sometimes prescribed for people with sore throats as well as being used in the treatment of lung infections. For most Sri Lankans, however, jaggery is their go-to sweetener with a taste similar to brown sugar (which is, therefore, a suitable substitute in recipes). In the villages, people often keep a small chunk of jaggery in their mouth while sipping tea instead of adding the sweetener directly to the beverage.

The syrup made from *kithul* sap, known as treacle, completes a popular dessert when poured over curd (yogurt).

Shymala's Coconut Custard Pudding

Wattalampan

A thicker, richer version of caramel pudding using coconut milk and jaggery, this dessert was introduced to Sri Lanka by Malay traders. My cousin Shymala makes an especially good version.

8 eggs
¾ pound (340 g) grated jaggery
2 cups (500 ml) thick coconut milk
1 tablespoon cornstarch

½ teaspoon grated nutmeg
¼ teaspoon cardamom powder
½ cup (125 ml) chopped cashews

1. Preheat oven to 350 degrees F (125 degrees C). Beats eggs in a medium bowl. Add the other ingredients and mix well.

2. Strain and pour into a stainless-steel mold, cover with tin foil, and cook in a double boiler in the oven for 30 to 45 minutes until set. (The water should not boil under it but simmer gently.)

3. Remove from heat and cool. Cover and refrigerate for 5 to 6 hours. Sprinkle with chopped cashews before serving.

MAKES 6 TO 8 SERVINGS

Leela's Legendary Milk Toffee

Despite the name, don't think hard English toffee or the chewy American kind. Leela, my Aunty Dora's cook of over forty years, often made this sweet dessert that crumbles easily and melts in your mouth. As it requires constant stirring, you get a bit of a workout while making it, too, so don't worry about indulging in the final product!

1 large can (525 g) sweetened
  condensed milk
2 cups water, poured into empty
  milk can first to get all its contents
2 tablespoons sugar

5 teaspoons butter, divided
1 teaspoon vanilla extract
¼ teaspoon cardamom powder
4 tablespoons cashews, chopped

1. Combine condensed milk, water, and sugar in a deep pan and stir until sugar is mostly dissolved.

2. Butter a half-sheet pan with 2 teaspoons butter and line with parchment paper then butter that as well.

3. Add 2 teaspoons butter to condensed milk mixture and cook on low heat, stirring constantly, until thick, about 30 minutes.

4. Add vanilla, cardamom powder, and 2 tablespoons cashews. Continue stirring for an additional 30 minutes until mixture darkens slightly and starts receding from the side of the pan when stirred.

5. Quickly pour onto prepared sheet pan to cool. Sprinkle with remaining cashews. Wait about 5 minutes and cut into squares while still hot.

Coconut Rock

This dessert is like a Mounds candy bar without the chocolate covering—just soft, chewy, sweet coconut.

2 pounds (1 kg) sugar
1 cup (250 ml) milk
1 pound (454 g) freshly grated or
  desiccated coconut

2 tablespoons chopped cashews
food coloring (optional)

1. In a small pan, dissolve sugar in milk and bring to a boil.

2. Add coconut and cook on medium heat, stirring constantly, until mixture leaves the sides of the pan.

3. Add cashews (and food coloring if desired) before removing from heat. Mix well.

4. Spread about 1-inch thick on a greased board and cut into squares while still hot. Cool before serving.

Rice Pudding

A British favorite imported to Sri Lanka during the time of its longest colonial rulers. This particular comfort food became an instant hit with the rice-loving Sri Lankans.

¼ pound (113 g) basmati rice
3½ cups (875 ml) water
1 small can (14 oz/396 g) sweetened
  condensed milk
¼ teaspoon ground cinnamon

½ teaspoon cardamom powder
¼ cup (65 ml) chopped cashews
  (optional)
¼ cup (65 ml) raisins or sultanas
  (optional)

1. Wash rice and cook in the water for 5 to 10 minutes.

2. Add condensed milk and bring to a boil. Reduce heat and simmer, stirring constantly, until mixture thickens, about 30 to 45 minutes.

3. Add cinnamon and cardamom powder. Remove from heat and pour into a bowl. Cool in fridge for 2 to 3 hours.

4. Garnish with cashews and raisins before serving if desired.

Sri Lankan Fruit Salad

Nothing soothes the soul after a heavy meal better than a light, cool, and fruity dessert. Serve with a dollop of ice cream, custard (page 219), or yogurt to take it up a notch.

1 small pineapple
1 small papaya
2 mangoes
2 bananas

1 tablespoon lemon juice
1 tablespoon sugar
¼ cup (85 g) shredded sweetened
  coconut

1. Peel and cut all fruits into bite-sized chunks. Combine in a bowl and sprinkle with lemon juice and sugar.

2. Cover with plastic wrap and place in fridge for 2 hours to chill.

3. Garnish with shredded coconut before serving.

Custard

No fruit salad or Christmas pudding is complete without this delicious topping.

1 can (14 oz/396 g) sweetened
  condensed milk
4 egg yolks
¼ cup (60 g) sugar

¼ teaspoon grated nutmeg
pinch of allspice
1 teaspoon vanilla extract

1. Pour condensed milk into a saucepan along with one can of water.

2. Beat the egg yolks. Add beaten yolks, sugar, nutmeg, and allspice into saucepan and stir well with wooden spoon over low heat. Continue stirring to avoid lumps until the spoon is thinly coated with custard. Remove from heat and keep stirring until custard is cool.

3. Add vanilla and chill in fridge before serving.

Christmas Pudding

One of the more lasting contributions by the British, Christmas pudding ranks as one of the richest desserts on the planet. Many Sri Lankans still celebrate Christmas, and the season would not be complete without this dessert. As a child, I used to love how my mother doused it with spirits and brought it flaming to the table to eat with either brandy sauce or custard.

2 cups (500 ml) brown raisins
2 cups (500 ml) white/golden raisins
1 cup (250 ml) currants
1 cup (250 ml) finely chopped
  candied fruit mix
1 cup (250 ml) finely chopped
  candied cherries
1 apple, peeled and grated
1 carrot, grated
1 cup (250 ml) chopped unsalted
  cashews
1 tablespoon finely grated lemon
  peel
1 tablespoon finely grated orange
  peel

juice of 1 lemon
juice of 1 orange
1 teaspoon cardamom powder,
  roasted
1 teaspoon ground cloves, roasted
1 teaspoon grated nutmeg
1 cup (250 ml) sherry
1 cup (250 ml) brandy
1 cup (250 ml) butter
1 cup (250 ml) packed brown sugar
6 eggs
4 cups (1 liter) fresh breadcrumbs
2 cups (500 ml) flour

1. In a deep bowl, combine all the fruits, carrots, nuts, peel, juices, spices, sherry, and brandy. Cover tightly and leave overnight.

2. On the following day, cream the butter and sugar together. Add eggs and beat well. Fold into fruit mixture. Fold in the breadcrumbs in parts alternating with the flour.

3. Fill two medium (2-quart) ceramic or stainless steel pudding bowls with mixture (2 inches from top) and cover each with 2 layers of parchment paper. Tie string around bowls so they are watertight. Cover with tin foil to further seal.

4. Place bowls in saucepans filled with hot water that will come a quarter of the way up the bowl. Steam puddings for 4 hours keeping water at a low boil and making sure that there is always enough water in the pans to cook them but not boil over.

5. Remove from heat and cool.

6. Remove original paper and cover with fresh parchment. Seal with foil. The pudding can be stored in a cool place for up to 6 months.

7. On Christmas Day, steam pudding for a further 2 hours and serve hot with custard (page 219) or brandy sauce.

Brandy Sauce

1¼ cups unsalted butter, softened
2 cups sifted confectioners' powdered sugar

1 teaspoon vanilla extract
4 tablespoons brandy or cognac

Mix butter, confectioners' sugar, vanilla, and brandy or cognac with an electric mixer until smooth. Place sauce in a serving bowl and refrigerate. Remove from fridge about one hour before serving.

Aunty Sita's Chocolate Biscuit Pudding

This scrumptious no-bake dessert is a contemporary Sri Lankan favorite. My Aunt Sita makes an incredibly wicked one.

1 pound (454 g) confectioner's powdered sugar
1 pound (454 g) cocoa powder
1 pound (454 g) unsalted butter, softened
2 teaspoons vanilla extract

splash of brandy (optional)
40 Goya Chocolate Maria cookies
1 cup (250 ml) milk
½ pound (226 g) roasted unsalted cashews, chopped

1. Mix confectioner's sugar, cocoa powder, butter, and vanilla together in a bowl to a creamy consistency. Add a splash of brandy if you like.

2. Coat a 9x13x4 Pyrex dish with butter.

3. Dip the cookies in milk and place in a single layer in the Pyrex dish.

4. Place a generous spoonful of the cocoa mixture on top, spreading it out evenly. Place a layer of chopped cashews on top of this. Continue layering until all ingredients are used.

5. Set in fridge for 2 to 3 hours before serving.

Baked Sago Pudding

Similar to chia seeds, sago seeds absorb liquid, becoming somewhat gelatinous when wet.

½ of a small can (from a 14 oz/396 g can) sweetened condensed milk
2 cups (500 ml) water
4 heaping tablespoons sago

pinch of salt
2 or 3 eggs, separated
dash of lemon juice

1. Heat oven to 350 degrees F (175 degrees C). Combine condensed milk, water, and sago in a medium pan and bring to a boil. Reduce heat and simmer until thick, about 30 to 45 minutes.

2. Mix in salt before removing pudding from heat. Allow to cool to room temperature.

3. Beat the egg yolks and stir into the pudding with the lemon juice. Beat the egg whites to soft peaks and fold into the pudding.

4. Pour pudding into buttered pie dish and bake for about 1 hour, until pudding is browned and set. May be served warm or cold.

King Yam Pudding
Rasawalli Pudding

You may not be able to source the purple King yams found in the north of the country, but any sweet yam will do. This dessert is quick, easy, and delicious.

1 pound (454 g) yams
2 cups (500 ml) coconut milk
1 cup (250 ml) coconut cream

4 ounces (113 g) sugar
salt to taste

1. Wash, peel and cut yams into thin slices.

2. Cook yams in a pan with coconut milk until soft, about 10 to 15 minutes.

3. Remove from heat and mash the yams with the back of a wooden spoon. Add coconut cream and sugar and bring to a boil, stirring often. Cook until all sugar has dissolved.

4. Serve hot or cold.

Coconut Sweetmeat
Kalu Dodol

This local specialty, somewhat akin to a fudge, requires patience and stamina (for the constant stirring), but your efforts are rewarded with a chewy, delicious sweet.

1 pound (454 g) jaggery (palm sugar)
3 ounces (85 g) cashews, chopped
6 cups (1.5 liters) coconut milk
½ teaspoon cardamom powder

4 ounces (113 g) rice flour
2 ounces (56 g) whole cashews (for garnish)

1. Grate the jaggery using a box grater.

2. Place jaggery in a large bowl with chopped cashews, coconut milk, and cardamom powder. Gradually mix in rice flour so there are no lumps.

3. Pour mixture into medium saucepan and cook over medium heat, stirring constantly until it thickens. As the mixture forms into a mass, oil will begin to form around the edges. Remove oil with a spoon, while continuing to stir.

4. When thickened, pour mixture into an 8x10 baking pan and let cool. Garnish with whole cashews, cut into squares, and serve.

Avocado Cream

Bet you've never enjoyed avocados for dessert! This old-school Sri Lankan treat was one of my grandfather's favorites. The simple and delicious preparation assumes the creamy texture of ice cream the longer you leave it in the freezer. The natural fat of avocados mimics the fat of heavy cream, but, of course, it's much healthier for you, so indulge!

2 ripe avocados
¼ cup condensed milk (or more if
  you like it sweeter)
1 teaspoon vanilla extract

1. Halve and pit avocados, removing the flesh to a bowl. Mash with a fork until they form a uniform paste.

2. Add condensed milk and vanilla and stir to incorporate until smooth.

3. Place in freezer for at least 6 hours and up to overnight.

4. Thaw slightly before serving like ice cream.

MAKES 2 SERVINGS

BEVERAGES

In a hot country, it's important to stay hydrated, so Sri Lankans enjoy a variety of hot and cold drinks to quench their thirst. Tea, an important legacy of British rule, is enjoyed island-wide, but so is iced coffee, made out of instant. All manner of tropical fruit juices are available at roadside stands along with the ubiquitous orange King Coconut, or *thambili,* which offer their refreshing, slightly sweet water when hacked open with a machete. Ginger beer is likely the most popular carbonated beverage while the liquor of choice is Arrack, distilled from the sap of coconut flowers.

Tea

Some of the best tea in the world is grown right here on this little island that the British fondly knew as Ceylon. Therefore, Sri Lankans take their tea seriously. While green tea has been cultivated more recently for its health benefits, the mainstay remains black tea, which has been dried and fermented. Since tea bags usually contain the sweepings of the factory floor, you should always buy loose tea and brew it properly in a teapot just like the Sri Lankans and, of course, the Brits do several times a day.

TO BREW TEA:

1. To a teapot add 1 teaspoon of loose tea leaves per person plus one for the teapot.

2. Fill the pot with boiling water, stir, and allow the tea leaves to settle and infuse, brewing for 2 to 3 minutes. The longer you brew it the stronger the cup of tea it yields.

3. Pour tea through a fine mesh strainer. Add milk and sugar to taste, or you can use condensed milk like the locals. Sometimes just a squeeze of lemon might do.

4. Drink while hot or cool it down to room temp and chill in the fridge for iced tea.

Iced Coffee

Before tea became the major cash crop in Sri Lanka, coffee ruled the interior highlands, and it is slowly reappearing. Previously, if you wanted a cup of coffee in Sri Lanka, you had to rely on Nescafe, the overwhelming favorite among islanders. But recently, the cultivation of coffee has been making a comeback. Sri Lanka still has a way to go to catch up to the taste and quality of a country like Vietnam's coffee, but even instant doesn't taste so bad when it's sweetened with the special ingredient—condensed milk.

1 to 2 teaspoons Nescafe (depending
   on how strong you like it) or ¼ cup
   espresso (about 2 shots)
Condensed milk to taste

FOR ONE CUP:

1. Boil water as if making a regular cup of coffee, but only add ¼ cup of it to a glass or cup along with the Nescafe. Add a teaspoon or 2 (or 3 or 4) of condensed milk and stir until dissolved.

2. Top up glass with cold water and ice cubes and stir well. Enjoy immediately or save in the fridge for later.

Ceylon Tea

With a reputation known far and wide, Ceylon tea has consistently been one of Sri Lanka's main exports, keeping pace on the international market even amongst competition from such larger producers as China and India. Today it stakes its claim as the only single origin tea in the world, as opposed to standard supermarket teas, which are a blend of leaves from thirty or more countries. Ceylon tea also remains the only variety still plucked by hand, and minimally processed.

Introduced in 1867 by British planter James Taylor, tea quickly replaced coffee as the thriving cash crop on the island following the scourge of *Hemileia Vastatrix* (Coffee Rust), a fungal disease that afflicted most of Sri Lanka's coffee plantations. Taylor's first cuttings, taken from Assam, India, took root at the Loolecondra Estate in Kandy in the island's central highlands, where low humidity, cool temperatures, and adequate rainfall provided the ideal climate for the crop. Between 1873 and 1880, tea production rose from just 23 pounds to 81.3 tons. By 1890 that number had reached 22,900 tons. Advancements in technology accompanied the steady rise of tea production so that by 1927, Sri Lanka was exporting over 100,000 metric tons of tea a year. That number doubled by 1965 making Sri Lanka the world's largest tea exporter.

Driving this production was a workforce of Indian Tamils—mostly women, whose smaller hands were considered better suited for the task of plucking leaves from the short bushes—initially brought over by the British to work the coffee plantations. Developing their own community distinct from Sri Lankan Tamils, these Indian Tamils, according to recent estimates, number around 300,000 today. If you take a trip to Sri Lanka's highlands you can see them dotting the teeming green slopes in brightly colored saris, filling the huge woven baskets on their backs with speed, grace, precision, and lots of tea leaves.

After being plucked, the bales of tea are brought to musk sheds, where they are weighed and undergo an initial inspection. From there the leaves proceed to an on-site factory where they are withered by large blowers. Then they are cut to release their juices, a key step that begins the fermentation process. Finally, the leaves are fired to lock in the flavor and dried.

For a tea to be designated as "Pure Ceylon Tea—Packed in Sri Lanka," it undergoes a rigorous inspection by the Sri Lanka Tea Board. The three grades of Sri Lankan tea are ranked according to the elevation at which they are grown.

High or Up-country (Udarata), characterized by its golden hue and intense flavor, is considered the best, followed by Mid-country (Medarata), and then Low-country. The latter, though lacking the distinctive flavor of higher grown teas, is still of good quality. There are further gradings based on size and appearance—namely "Leaf" grades, such as Orange Pekoe (OP) and "Broken" grades such as Broken Orange Pekoe Fannings (BOPF).

Fermented Ginger Beer

A well-respected company called Elephant House makes the commercially-available, carbonated ginger beer that is enjoyed all over the island. But I prefer making my own, which, in addition to being less sweet, has the added benefit of being naturally effervescent from the fermentation, therefore making it much healthier for you as well. This recipe requires some patience and commitment, but once you have produced the ginger bug—similar to a sourdough starter—you can enjoy refreshing, homemade ginger beer whenever you like. If tending the ginger bug becomes a chore, you can always cover it and put it into hibernation in the fridge.

GINGER BUG:

2 cups (500 ml) filtered water
6 tablespoons granulated white
  sugar

6 tablespoons washed and grated
  ginger root
cheesecloth

1. Combine water, 2 tablespoons white sugar, and 2 tablespoons ginger root in a 1-quart glass or plastic container. Mix well until sugar is fully dissolved. Cover with cheesecloth, label, and date, and let sit on the counter for 24 hours.

2. Add the same amount of ginger and sugar to the container every 24 hours until it becomes fizzy, which should take about 2 to 3 days. Once you see those tiny bubbles forming you are ready to make ginger beer.

GINGER BEER:

2 quarts (1.90 liters) filtered water
1¼ cups granulated white or brown
  sugar

¼ cup washed and grated ginger
  root
juice of 3 lemons or limes

1. Place all ingredients (except the citrus) in a large pot. Simmer for 5 to 8 minutes on low heat until the sugar is dissolved. Then let cool to room temp.

2. Pour mixture into a bowl through a fine-mesh strainer, and make sure to press out all the liquid.

3. Add ½ cup of strained ginger bug and the lemon or lime juice and stir well.

4. Transfer ginger beer to flip-top bottles, leaving about 2-inches headroom. Close bottles and let sit on counter for 3 to 6 days until fizzy to your liking. **NOTE:** You will have to 'burp' these bottles every day for a couple minutes to release the build-up of gases. (Caution: Failure to do so might cause the bottles to explode.)

5. Place in fridge to stop fermentation and enjoy at your leisure.

Lime Juice

The limes in Sri Lanka are tiny and do not yield much juice, so this recipe is based on the bigger limes available in the west. Choose limes that are firm but still have some give. Roll them on a flat surface beneath the palm of your hand to loosen them up before juicing. Then cut them in half and twist a spoon through the flesh to extract the most juice. But the real twist to this recipe lies in the addition of a little salt and pepper, which might sound strange, but adds a lot of complexity to this simple refresher.

Juice of 6 to 10 limes
Sugar to taste
water
salt & pepper to taste

1. Add ⅓ cup lime juice, about 1 teaspoon of sugar, and some salt and pepper to taste to a glass.

2. Dilute with cold water, add ice cubes, and stir to mix well. Adjust any flavors that need it—adding more sugar or salt.

VARIATION: LIME SODA
Add carbonated water instead of regular water in step 2.

Faluda

Originally a Persian dessert called *faloodeh*, this cloyingly sweet drink spread across Asia through the conquests of the Mughal empire, based in what is today Pakistan. Every country has their own take on it, and Sri Lanka is no exception. The basic recipe, however, involves some combination of rose syrup, vermicelli, sweet basil seeds (otherwise known as sabja or tukmaria seeds), and milk with ice cream being optional. The rose syrup (not to be confused with rose water or rose essence) and sweet basil seeds may be hardest to procure in the US but should be available online at any site selling Indian products.

4 tablespoons rose syrup
1⅓ cups milk
2 tablespoons sweet basil seeds,
  soaked in water for 30 minutes
2 tablespoons cooked vermicelli
  noodles (optional)

2 scoops vanilla ice cream
1 tablespoon chopped pistachios
  (optional)
Rose petals (optional)

1. To assemble, use two 12-ounce glasses. Add 2 tablespoons of rose syrup to each glass, followed by ⅔ cup milk. Stir well to incorporate.

2. To each glass add 1 tablespoon of soaked sweet basil seeds and 1 tablespoon vermicelli (if using).

3. Top off with a scoop of vanilla ice cream and garnish with pistachios or rose petals.

MAKES 2 SERVINGS

Fruit Shakes

A blender and some ice are all it takes to convert the tropical goodness of Sri Lanka into a delicious and cooling beverage. For pineapple, mango, or guava you can even use overripe fruits, which tend to be sweeter. For a coconut shake, simply use canned coconut milk.

¾ cup of chopped fruit (pineapple, mango, or guava); or 1 cup coconut milk

¼ cup orange juice or water (omit for coconut shake)

1 cup ice cubes

Sugar to taste

Place all ingredients into blender and blend until smooth. Pour contents into a glass and enjoy.

SAMPLE RICE & CURRY MENUS

Rice & Curry meals are served all together, buffet-style so diners may pick and choose from a variety of meat, fish, and vegetable dishes. In addition to the curries, there is usually at least one chutney or pickle; a fresh salad; and papadum (crispy, wafer-thin chips made from lentil flour that is deep-fried, available at any Indian store). When putting together a menu, attention should be paid to the interplay of colors, textures, and flavors, which will ultimately be presented and eaten together. Pay extra attention to the amount of chili you use when preparing these curries so as not to lose any guests along the way and be sure to include mild dishes along with the spicier ones.

MENUS FOR 4 TO 6 PEOPLE

Sri Lankan Basic Rice (page 86)
Chicken Curry (page 109) or Shrimp Curry (page 135)
Sri Lankan Lentils (page 145)
Mallung (page 151)
Eggplant Curry (page 158)
Coconut Sambol (page 201)

Ghee Rice (page 87)
Beef Curry (page 111) or Red Fish Curry (page 136)
Spiced Potatoes (page 162)
Moong Bean Curry (page 157)
Okra Curry (page 161)
Onion Chili Sambol (page 202)

VEGETARIAN
Yellow Rice (page 88)
French Green Bean Curry (page 154)
Carrot Curry (page 146)
Chickpea Curry (page 172)
Tomato Cucumber Salad (page 207)
Bitter Gourd Sambol (page 204)

MENUS FOR 6 TO 8 PEOPLE

Sri Lankan Basic Rice (page 86)
Lamb Curry (page 112) or Pork Curry (page 110)
Crab Curry (page 132) or Squid Curry (page 131)
Cabbage Curry (page 169)
Potato Curry (page 147)
Mallung (page 151)
Carrot Sambol (page 203)

Yellow Rice (page 88)
Sour Fish Curry (page 140)
Chicken Liver, Pea & Cashew Curry (page 114)
Sri Lankan Lentils (page 145)
Sauteed Leeks (page 170)
Radish & Tomato Sambol (page 203)

VEGETARIAN
Vegetable Fried Rice (page 92)
Soya Curry (page 173)
Yellow Pumpkin Curry (page 176)
Mushroom Curry (page 168)
Spinach Curry (page 150)
Beetroot Curry (page 148)
Tomato Cucumber Salad (page 207)

MENUS FOR 8 TO 10 PEOPLE

Sri Lankan Basic Rice (page 86)
Chicken Curry (page 109) or Pork Curry (page 110)
Beef Curry (page 111) or Lamb Curry (page 112)
Deviled Shrimp or Squid (page 68)
Sri Lankan Lentils (page 145)
French Green Bean Curry (page 154)
Mallung (page 151)
Fish Cutlets (page 57)
Coconut Sambol (page 201)

Yellow Rice (page 88) or Ghee Rice (page 87)
Fish Mustard Curry (page 139) or Deviled Shrimp (page 68)
Mutton Curry (page 112) or Deviled Beef (page 67)
Mushroom Curry (page 168)
Eggplant Curry (page 158)
Cauliflower Curry (page 178)
Mango Curry (page 175)
Carrot Sambol (page 203)

RESOURCES

Online sites for Sri Lankan products and groceries:

USA: Grocerylanka.com
Flavorsofceylon.com
Lakfood.com
Ceylontropicalhut.com
Skizsoriginal.com

CANADA: Ceylongroceries.com
Srilankanroots.com

RICE & CURRY INDEX

ABOUT THE AUTHOR

S.H. ("SKIZ") FERNANDO JR. is a second-generation Sri Lankan-American and graduate of Harvard University and the Columbia University School of Journalism. As a journalist, he has written for *The New York Times, Rolling Stone, Lucky Peach,* and *Saveur.* In 2006, he moved to Sri Lanka for a year to learn about its cuisine and to research this cookbook. He has been featured on NPR and the Travel Channel's *No Reservations with Anthony Bourdain,* where he led the crew to Sri Lanka's best food spots in March 2009. He offers Sri Lankan supper clubs, his own line of spices, and tours of the island at www.skizsoriginal.com.